Dying Education: Necessary Reformation. The Nigerian Case

Dying Education: Necessary Reformation. The Nigerian Case

Ezeoke, Alphonsus Emeka

iUniverse, Inc.
Bloomington

Dying Education: Necessary Reformation. The Nigerian Case

iUniverse books may be ordered through booksellers or by contacting:

iUniverse
1663 Liberty Drive
Bloomington, IN 47403
www.iuniverse.com
1-800-Authors (1-800-288-4677)

ISBN: 978-1-4620-5159-5 (sc)
ISBN: 978-1-4620-5161-8 (hc)
ISBN: 978-1-4620-5160-1 (ebk)

Printed in the United States of America

iUniverse rev. date: 08/26/2011

CONTENTS

Dedication

To the growth of education in Nigeria and to all lovers of education, especially the Youth and Children who struggle to learn and be educated.

Acknowledgement

I thank God who made it possible for me to have the decorum to write this book and who has continued to be with his unworthy servant. I want to thank my siblings for their continued support and exemplary Christian life. To my mom, you are like an angel to us, may God continue to guide you. I thank you mom. To my late father Sylvester Enendu Ezeoke (KSM—Eziokwu bu Ndu) who sacrificed all he had for the education of his children, may God reward you with eternal bliss? I miss you.

To my bishop, Most Rev. Dr. Paulinus C. Ezeokafor, thank you for your support and the opportunity of time for my sabbatical leave. I want to thank Most Rev. Dr. Simon A. Okafor (Bishop Emeritus of Awka) for his support and encouragement. To Mrs. Cathy Grandjean MA BCC (erstwhile Director, Catholic Health Services of Long Island), and Rev. Fr. Polycarp C. Nnajiofor PhD, thank you for taking the pains to proof read my work and being there when I needed your attention. To Prof Gerald Cattaro, thank you for the Foreward to this book and for your good disposition. Thank you Very Rev. Msgr. J.P.C. Nzomiwu for the comment at the back of the book. I want to thank my colleagues in Long Island New York Rev. Fr Benet Uwasomba PhD and Rev Fr. Anthony Nwachukwu PhD for their support and good working relationship. To my good friends, thank you for being supportive and critical.

To all lovers of good education, be not disillusioned but continue with the knowledge and the information you have to better the world. Life is a continuum and could be made better with our contributions at this moment in history.

God bless you all
Emeka A. Ezeoke (Fr.)

Foreword

The struggle for proper education is a global concern as the international sphere and community of nations continues to be linked to one another whether the nation is one which is highly developed or still struggling to develop itself. Thus the struggle for proper education in Nigeria becomes a concern for all interested in the promotion of free societies. The struggle in Nigeria for educational equity and excellence is richly depicted in this elegant tome by Alphonsus Emeka Ezeoke. It is a well-heeled journey enabling the reader to investigate, explore and form judgements as to the development and practice of instruction in a nation which is rich in cultural constructs integral to education in any society yet a country which is bankrupt in models of accessible education for all children. This is self evident as he develops the thesis to promote necessary educational reform in his home country of Nigeria, a nation which engages in constant educational debates.

The particular style of writing pays attention to historical development allowing the reader to enjoy an anthropologically exploration of education in Nigeria revealing layer upon layer of complexity thus simplifying what would normally be for the first time student of Nigerian education a labyrinth. Dr. Ezeoke not only examines the ontology related to education in his homeland but the axiology of educational development thus providing the reader with a scholarly and serious work. Dr Ezeoke takes us to a place which is at first uncomfortable exploring social justice issues as he addresses the various problems inherent in a system which is plagued by tribalism and territorialism. Power who possesses it and how it is wielded seems to be at the heart of the challenge to the educational venue in Nigeria. Nigerian nation seems to be encoded by the complexities of imperialism which survived by encouraging existing historical feuds of various indigenous cultures against each other thus pitting brother against brother.

Dr Alphonsus Emeka Ezeoke received his formal training at Fordham University in New York, a Jesuit institution of Higher education. His major concentration was on Educational policy particularly as it pertains to developing nations. His studies included the publication of a thesis on comparative governance structure of schools office in United States and Nigerian education, allowing him the privilege to gain academic authority on this topic.

It is my hope that all who read what is contained in the chapters become agents of educational reform and change not only for Nigeria but for developing nations. The struggle for those engaged in the educational reform movements are not struggles of isolation but struggles of community to bring the world together so that all children are afforded the proper means to liberation and cultural Identity which is the power of education. Dying is only meaningful if there is a resurrection.

Prof. Dr. Gerald M. Cattaro
Chair
Educational Leadership Administration Policy
Graduate School of Education
Fordham University NY, USA

Introduction

Education in Nigerian is crumbling. It is sad to say this of a country with personalities of repute in academic, political, science and social fields. What has actually gone wrong in the Nigerian polity? The dying education has affected Nigeria greatly to an extent that death of education is imminent and the collapse of the nation not too far. The only recourse to revive this pending danger is reformation of the education sector and good leadership.

Education is a gift to humanity, bringing minds together in knowledge, understanding and operations. Education is significant to the development of the self, promotion of knowledge, skills acquisition, value orientation, more so, growth of a country and necessary for global interaction. The fruits of education have led to information age, securing order in the world and constant conquering of the universe. 'Education is the most powerful weapon which you can use to change the world' said Nelson Mandela. Education disposes the individual minds to learn, meet, grow, criticize, develop, accept, resolve, agree, build on research and relate with the other person, community, society, and the international body. To neglect education in any country is to deprive the country of life sustenance. A nation pays dearly when the education sector is not properly constituted, managed and funded. The lack of education is the lack of information, economic, political, social, and human development in any government or country. Education remains the bedrock to all successes, be it personal, group, community, government or nation.

Education in Nigeria cannot be complete without some historical background of the country. Education the way it is today in Nigeria is imported; it is not indigenous to the nation. This does not remove the fact that traditional education is gradually finding its place in Nigeria. It goes with the saying that when cultures meet, a cultural contact is made and cultural change evolves in the process with modification to the status quo. The greatest tool to development is education and this tool has been used by many to achieve their stated goals. Fafunwa, A. Babs (1995) accedes to the fact that, "every society, whether simple or complex, has its own system for training and educating its youth, and education for the good life has been one of the most persistent concerns of men throughout history" (p. 1). One laments the deplorable level to which Nigerian education has degenerated to, beginning with the failure of educational system to its infrastructural decay, under funding, unqualified teachers and understaffing of schools/institutions, lack of academic facilities/ equipments and no proper research facilities mingled with high rate of poverty and corruption. To deny these facts would be to betray the genuineness of the reality on ground and to resist change for a better future. There is urgent need for reformation of the education sector with the present appalling condition.

Nigeria became an independent country in October 1, 1960. Thus, recording over fifty years of age with all its appurtenances, yet its education which is the key to any country's growth has yet to come to standard and have its resources tapped. Nigeria is the most populous nation in Africa with a projected population of 166 million people, covering a land mass of 923.8 sq. km (356.700 sq. mi). Chief Samu'ila Danko Makama, the Chairman National Population Commission (NPC) confirms that, "by October 31 this year (2011), Nigeria's population is expected to hit 166 million mark just as the world population is projected to rise to seven billion from six billion" (Guardian News, 12 July 2011). However, BBC News on Nigeria country profile gave a UN (2010) figure for Nigerian population as 158.2 million. In a recent document by the

U.S. Department of State, titled "Background Note on Nigeria", the country's literacy level is between 31 percent and 51 percent. In a further analysis, secondary school attendance for the male population is recorded at 32 percent while that of female population is only 27 percent. Earlier, the federal ministry of education's 25-28 November 2008 National Report for the Forty-Eight session of the International Conference on Education (ICE) clearly says that:

> *Nigeria is the only E9 country in sub-Saharan Africa with equally the highest illiteracy rate in the sub-region.*
> *(Executive summary p .i)*

The Federal Republic of Nigeria is located in the Western part of the African continent. It has thirty-six states with the capital situated at Abuja. Nigeria has over two hundred and fifty (250) ethnic groups, with an outstanding three ethnic groups namely Igbo in the East, Yoruba in the West and Hausa in the North. Not only this, it has about three hundred and ninety four (394) languages, with English as its lingua franca. Falola Toyin (1999) adds that, "the country was divided into three big regions, North, West, and East, dominated by the Hausa-Fulani, Yoruba, and Igbo respectively. The three regions and their ethnicities competed as enemies" (p. 10).

Nigeria practices a 6-3-3-4 system of education. Every average child of the country is expected to spend a minimum of sixteen years in school. Six years of primary education, three years of junior secondary school, three years of senior secondary school and four years of higher education (university, college of education, or polytechnic). Nigeria operates both public and private schools. All schools owned by the government are public. All schools owned by individuals, groups, and religious bodies are private. Except for the private schools that cut across all school levels, Local government takes care of primary schools' education, State government controls secondary schools' and some tertiary institutions' education, while Federal government takes care of tertiary institutions' and some designated secondary schools' education. School period has continued to move from September to June and from January to

December. The inconsistency in pining down academic programme to a particular period is the uncontrolled incessant strikes by government workers and irresponsibility of government to dialogue effectively with workers. In between this twelve calendar months are holiday periods. Previous practice was from September to August with its holidays well built in. Today, strikes and demands have left the school calendar years indeterminate.

There is no doubt that Nigeria has a chequered history. The 1914 amalgamation of seemingly different sects of people by the Colonials has not helped education in the country. However, here is Nigeria and what next, or should the citizens continue to cry over an issue that should be thrown over board. Some nations have diverse people of different cultures, religion, language, beliefs and race, and yet they co habit effectively. The problem significant in Nigeria is its inability to openly discuss issues that separate the multi ethnic and dialectic people of the country, proffer solution to their differences and move on as a nation endowed with numerous gifts. No doubt the educational pattern and growth of these ethnic oriented peoples are different, but it is not different from many other countries. The nomads in the north, the traders in the south, all have perspective on education and what it can afford them. True to the fact is that the country has not been bereft of seeking to find solution but is bereft of the consciousness of ethnic multiplicity that shaped it. This body is education itself, and if properly studied and harnessed will boost development and the standard of living in Nigeria.

A factor that cannot be glossed over is the destructive military regime in Nigerian history. For a period of about thirty years, Nigeria was under military rule and dictatorship that crippled its education. Ogunmola, Dele and Badmus, and Isiaka Alani write that:

> *Apart from the fact that military rule is characterised by lack of transparency, accountability, and good governance 'much of the failure of policy and the lack of development have been attributed to the abnormal situation where a country was denied democracy and the rule of law, but rather was forcibly subjected to military misrule'. (p. 3).*

Beginning with the government takeover of schools after the Civil War in the 1970s, the military regime undermined the importance of education. It was a takeover of school with no harnessed system of education which brought decadence, corruption, marginalization and acrimony in the country. Not only that education had a gradual disappearance during the Civil War, it was murdered shortly after the Civil War. Nasir El-rufai (2011) categorically states "things went relatively well until the civil war. By 1970, shortly after the war, a period designated for reconstruction by the Federal Government, a few things occurred, which subsequently opened the floodgates drowning education today". Within the protracted military rule, there were a series of riots and strikes resulting in a decline in quality of educational system. Nigeria has not so much grown out of this embattled predicament to date. The shadow of the past has continued to estrange the people of the nation. In the 'First Catholic Education Summit in Nigeria', among other things, the Catholic Bishops Conference of Nigeria (2006) aptly stated:

> *4   That the forceful take-over of Church-owned and Church- managed schools in several States of the country over thirty-six years ago had significantly contributed to the unfortunate decline in [of] education in Nigeria.*
>
> *5   That this development, just at the end of the Nigerian civil war, caused a major dislocation in educational development in many States of the Federation. (p. 7)*

The graphic structure of education in Nigeria has never had a consistent growth. Though one may argue on the seeming changes in lieu of educational acts by the government but those were never guaranteed as registered growth. After all the Nigerian people are still waiting to see the impart of a national policy on education that led to the takeover of all primary and secondary schools previously owned by the private sector. More so, the education policies in the 1970s, the misuse of the oil boom, and the spending cuts in education especially in the late 1980s have intrinsically uprooted the educational base of the country. Further, the education sector is not bothered that about four hundred thousand students would qualify for higher education and only half of them could secure admission. Or, that about eight thousand students would sit for Joint Admission and Matriculation Board (JAMB) examination with half of them not getting up to half of the score to pass them. Again, some may allude that with the stability in democratic process in the country, education is beginning to wear a new look, yet there are pointers to educational mishap. The pathetic situation today is the percentage increase in schools enrolment at all levels of education but with high percentage poor performance. More explorations need to be made to secure good standard and find a way to wriggle out of borrowed robes. There are handicaps inhibiting academic growth and good education formation in Nigeria. Secondly, the current educational process in the country does not encourage productivity where even the educated people are in majority consumers and not producers. The unsaid fact is that consumers purchase the goods of others while producers have ownership of the product. Education is the greatest force of change for any nation. The social purposes of education is manifold including social control, improving social conditions, and reducing social tensions caused by economic inequalities (Ezeoke, A. E, 2003, p. 64). Ezeoke, Alphonsus E. (2003) went further to assert that, "when everybody receives the same education, and/or is given the equal opportunity, it cuts across the inequalities as seen today in our society" (p. 64).

Due to the fact that there are no challenging opportunities provided to the educated in Nigeria to excel, their counterpart in the Western and Asian world who smartly provide academic opportunities, make away with Nigerian children and their indigenous talent. These withdrawn personnel are not fully baked yet, but with the developmental technologies and information available to them abroad, they are turned into great producers (educationists, scientists, archaeologists, historians, legal gurus, industrialists, computer geniuses, great physicians, and experts in many other fields of life). Nigeria has continued to lose with the absence of these multi-talented individuals.

When a nation invests in education, it has made the best of all investments that can ever be. The nation's education is at crossroad, it is either we shove our differences under the carpet and call for a unity conference or do not build the nation. The crisis of education in Nigeria is to be addressed, if this generation has any legacy to leave for the younger generation. The fruit of education is the bond of a nation. Starratt, R. J. (1996) in a holistic way said:

> *I believe that an educated person is a person who tries to understand, appreciate, critique, and participate in his or her culture, traditions, and history. Such a person is also one who can participate in the public life of the community, who understands the political and social mechanism by which the community governs itself, and who handles the necessities of everyday life competently. (p. 6)*

In this 21st century, the country's needed development will come when ideas are tackled, shared and worked out. Only when the nation steps up to this level will it become informed and a re-orientation would automatically take place. Nigeria is a country of talents, endowed with the potentials to make great things and be reckoned as such. As the Sun News editorial affirms:

> *For Nigeria to become one of the 20 most industrialized nations of the world by the year 2020, we must widen access to university education, which is currently below expectation. What this amounts to is that government must increase funding of the education sector to take care of its inadequacies. The current funding is far below the 26 percent recommended by the United Nations Educational, Scientific and Cultural Organization (UNESO).*

Nigerian people are suffering and the great promise that once called out to this beloved nation cannot be heard amidst the chaos and insecurity circling it. There is need to regain ownership that now languishes on the vine. The author laments and puts this book out as a part to intervene now for the country's survival that is at stake. The writer invites you to share these words of John F. Kennedy:

> *Let us think of education as the means of developing our greatest abilities, because in each of us there is a private hope and dream which fulfilled, can be translated into benefit for everyone and greater strength for our nation.*

Education in Nigeria is dying. Unless something is done to reform this sector, it may not rise again.

Chapter One
Confused Situation/Position of Education

Education in Nigeria has been a debacle, overtly unplanned intermingled with instability of the nation. Under the colonials, education was mainly a process to get to understand a people being governed. The colonials made all effort to educate some people as to have an easier communication to ensure their trade and business manipulations. A lot of odds went into it as Warrant Chiefs (unpopular persons appointed by the Colonials) took seats of governance in traditionally settled people, other than the traditional chieftains. As more people turn to learn and understand the colonial mentality, there was no formal education established as such. Obtainable then were educational styles suitable to get the colonial regime to prosper. As the need to deepen relationship between Colonials and traditional kingdoms arose, proper education has to be in place. Fortunately there arose an opportunity for some people to be trained abroad by the colonials or missionaries that accompanied them. As little number of scholars began to emerge, coming back home to help form the government, establish educational system and seek for independence, Second World War broke out infringing on the gradual academic growth of a young nation, the protectorate of Nigeria.

The struggle for education has ever since the coming of the British and missionaries continued to grow unabated. The beginnings were always very hard, but surely education came to be valued by very few people. It has always been viewed then as Whiteman's continual game of subjugation. Other people consider it colonial domination and intrusion that must be carefully followed. With many factors that brought the tribes and multi ethnic groups together as Nigeria take shape, and as Nigeria won its independence, a new day dawned. This new day did not last long as coup and counter coup destroyed the fabric of the young nation. The dream of a good educational system became a mere shadow. Important to note and indeed a fact is, some years before and couple of years after independence marked stability in the education sector in Nigeria. At this stage in the Nigerian history, the country has growing awareness of education and produced brilliant and durable manpower on which the nation depended. Things were going as nicely as possible as the ethnic groups begin to understand each other and move the economic, sociological, technological and educational system forward. Education was at its best, with no riots or any form of interference to put it on hold until the period of coup d'êta. Many coups and counter coups brought set back in the education sector. Consequent to these coups, Civil War broke out and the education sector suffered and went into oblivion. It is amazingly true that, "in those days, Nigeria spent an average of 40 percent of her budget on education" (Nasir E, 2011). What possible answer can the Federal Government give to this budgetary decline in education? Nasir E. (2011) summarizes further

> *The budgetary attitude to education is yet to recover from this reversal of fortunes. Since 2007, Nigeria spent an average of about 0.7% of GDP and about 3% of the budget on education—among the lowest five ranked countries in the world!*

Military rule brought such disintegration that today the nation is still struggling to find its feet. Reminiscence of coup events, civil war, and government takeover of schools has generated so much mistrust. And there is a general lax, misguided opportunists, severed and battered people, that a once booming education sector could no longer find its feet in the complex society. The cost of the Civil War marred the progress of the Nigerian education.

i. The tripartite squabble, the metamorphosis

The squabble among the three prominent ethnic groups in Nigeria left the nation's educational system in shambles. The ethnic groups in question are Igbo, Hausa and Yoruba. There was no proper harnessing of this three power ethnic groups before the amalgamation of Nigeria in 1914 by the British as 'Colony and Protectorate of Nigeria'. Bickering and rancour, hostility at a great magnitude and squabble in its highest form posed great danger to day to day living and governance in the country. But one thing good about it is that individuals from the prominent ethnic areas were challenged to gain more education than the other which gives credence to the notion that knowledge is power. Clever ones had the opportunity to quickly study abroad where the system of education was more stable and would give them more clout in the society. Back in the country, major universities of the three ethnic groups were in competition viz., University of Ibadan of Yoruba ethnic land, University of Nsukka of Igbo ethnic land and Ahmadu Bello University of Hausa ethnic land. Healthy academic rivalry is good, but bitterness as to who is superior and who should be prima facie in government and politics is bad as this promotes an unhealthy spirit and opens the door to unnecessary bickering and undermining of knowledge and ability. This attitude has ever since continued, as each looks down on the other not minding whatever good that may arise from the other.

The tripartite structure representing the three key ethnic groups became more visible in October 1, 1960, when Nigeria became a Federation of Three Regions namely, Northern, Western and Eastern. Correspondingly therefore, Northern region belongs to the Hausa tribe, Western region to the Yoruba tribe, and Eastern region to the Igbo tribe. Each of these regions has many ethnic groups that make them up. This structure provided for the Parliamentary form of government introduced by the British. Pertinent to this is that the regions retained some measure of autonomy via self government. When the military coups and counter coups, take-over and retake-over of the country Nigeria continued, Lt. Colonel Yakubu Gown emerged as the Military Head of State. In the bid to quickly restructure Nigeria as the Head of State, he created Twelve States out of the three regions in the country. This plan of action was rejected by the Governor of the Eastern Region Lt. Colonel Emeka Odimegwu Ojukwu. Lt. Colonel Emeka Odimegwu Ojukwu and the Easterners did not recognize Lt. Colonel Yakubu Gown as the General Military Head of State after the blood coup that led to his ascendance, and more especially as it revised the structural Regions to States in May 27 1967 without conventional conference of the Federation. Subsequent Civil War emerged as the Easterners persisted on secession of the Eastern region in May 30 1967 for the state of Biafra led by its Regional Military Governor Lt. Col. Emeka Ojukwu.

The colossal effect of military regime and of the civil war was the demise of education. The center could no longer hold as mistrust ensued among the three key ethnic groups. Each major tribe Igbo, Hausa and Yoruba thinks it can survive alone but the history of the nation has proved them wrong. Attempts have been made by each of these major ethnic groups to sidetrack each other. The education sector suffers the same malaise until a common ground is sought. Just as military policies were antithetical to educational growth so is the tripartite squabble a cancerous disease in the nation's growth.

ii. Certificate Syndrome

This is very difficult to discuss because today Nigerian society is crazed about obtaining certificates. Apparently, it is the major tool to ascertain qualification. It cannot be stressed more that there are certificates for those who want them in every nook and cranny of the globe. It suffices today that what people do is to learn enough to

4

obtain a certificate. There is no in-depth knowledge; people's needs are just pay increases, promotion, and big offices simply because there is certificate to present. Today, the demand to present your resume or Curriculum Vitae (CV) is more linked to certificates one can produce. What this does is that it projects certificate more than a person's actual work experience and accomplishments. The fact being expressed therefore is that it is not the experience that counts but if the individual holds a required certificate from a recognized institution. The incredible situation tends to be that experience has no grounds in the face of certificate. Precisely why our system is partly collapsing as Nigerian academia is still battling on how best to ascertain the credibility of some of these certificates. Certificates are meant to enhance an area of study and are not meant to replace higher education degrees. One reason why our system is partly collapsing is this rush for certificates by Nigerian academia.

This craze for certificates in Nigeria has given the work force both negative and positive embellishment. As some have really worked very hard to take up jobs and ascended to position of greatness, others have manipulated the system to get to their positions which is most often unnoticed. Reference to today's Information Technology (IT) and award of certificates seem to approve any computer house as a certificate institution. The point here is that a lot of individuals appear to look for a quick fix to become certified. More so, a lot of people claim to be university, polytechnic and college of education graduates but they did not pass through the walls of any tertiary institutions. Some do forge certificates, and unfortunately, they are mostly undetected. Provision of one's transcript/s may help to check-mate some of these ill begotten certificates in work places and institutions.

One still wonders, in the midst of this certificate syndrome, the rightful place of experience or field work in a productive circle. Certification based on in-service training builds on acquired knowledge and gears towards better productivity. Experience needs to be compared with certificate to balance productivity. In effect, experience validates certification. It is not sufficient to claim I have the certificate, rather, that I am capable to take up task requisite to my position. In view of this, the hiring process needs to recognize clear knowledge of the subject matter and the employer should really probe and determine how in-depth the skills of the acclaimed individuals are. The Nigerian hiring bodies need to develop a systemic way to process certificates and experience in general. In an interview granted to Dike Gabriel and Otti Sam, the National Examination Council registrar Mr Okpala decried that, "certificate forgery is becoming a problem that is not just worrying only NECO but the entire education sector".

People have argued that school knowledge has no bearing on what happens in the real world. The point made is not all wrong from the development of things in the country. In some academic programs, there is a lack of practical knowledge where students can actually see for themselves the extent of their knowledge base. What this does is to help impact on knowledge retention, and for those on in-service training to improve in job performance. In some cases then, certification may not be the problem but rather the certification training process. It is important that we do this in Nigeria especially since these practices have all dissipated.

In fairness this is not a condemnation of all certificates as it is overtly, a clearer way to strategize qualification. Certificate is an indication that one has a baseline level of knowledge and is able to demonstrate acquired knowledge by passing the examination. This process requires some number of years depending on the nature of academic program. It is disheartening when cut and join games are found in some academic fields and rips the society of qualified personnel. To see educationists succumbing to anything goes for want of money or greed is a colossal failure in the academic world.

iii. Online Academic Business

Online learning is an academic programme of study that has come to stay. The American Federation of Teachers has had a series of in-depth studies on this with its attendant pros and cons. It is believed that, the methods and styles of online education evolved greatly to accommodate difficulties of people who cannot undergo classroom education. Yet today technology and its manipulations have left the society bereft of the true nature of things. Or is it that today technology is leading us to a totally new world and all are griped with fear of the unknown. The tangible but complex truth is that there is a surge of young people choosing non-traditional education as means to commence, grow and advance in careers, as they complete their basic and formal education. The question becomes at what point can online education provide access for proper academic growth? Is online education proper for first degree, masters, professional studies and doctoral programmes?

There are still strong arguments both for and against online learning or, distance learning. This follows the saying that there is no one best way to learn. The following is a study by the American Federation of Teachers in 2001, on 'A Virtual Revolution: Trends in the Expansion of Distant Education'. The key interest is on tables 2 and 3, where the advantages and disadvantages are spelt out. Important to note in this study would be, to what degree is this online learning applicable in Nigeria, and to Nigerians who would practice and produce in the country?

Table 2: Nominations of Pros (Advantages) of Online Learning Rank Pros (Advantages) of online learning named and Number of Nominations

1   Flexibility of time to work; work at own pace (any time of day, even on busy schedule) 135
2   Save time on travel to/from campus; parking hassles. 74
3   Convenience; freedom; accessible any time, from anywhere. 68
4   More resources available for the course; easy access to course materials. 59
5   Learn new technology / up-to-date developments, Internet skills. 54
6   Instructor more accessible; quick answers to questions; help available 24 hours 40

7   More comfortable to work at home or place of my choice 32

8   Allows more time to think before answering questions 29

9   Saves money on gasoline, childcare, car, and housing. 25

10 More peer / class interaction; more personal or meaningful communication 22

11 Can review material often 22

12 Non-threatening atmosphere; reduces stress; less anxiety or worry (e.g. being late for class). 20

13 Learn to be more focused, self-motivated, independent, or disciplined 18

14 Interacting with students all over the world 14

15 Clearer or more effective communication with my classmates 14

16 No worry about how to dress; PJs to class. 13

17 More interaction, collaboration, or sharing of ideas 13

18 Avoid boring or unpleasant classes or classmates 11

19 Fits my learning style 11

20 More flexible, varied, dynamic instruction: interactive, hands-on; non-textbook 11

21-37 Other themes (17) with fewer than 10 nominations each 63

Total nominations: 747

Table 3: Nominations of Cons (Disadvantages) of Online Learning
Rank Cons (Disadvantages) of online learning named and Number of Nominations

1   Lack of face-to-face, personal or social contact with instructor or students 126

2   Technical Problems (including computer, server, network, power), or fear of technical problems 83

3   Requires too much self-discipline, self-motivation, time-management and organization 79

4   Technical / computer literacy or keyboarding /typing skills and comfort level required. 63

5   Communication, directions, or discussions are unclear or more difficult or confusing 45

6   Lack of immediate help or feedback 31

7   Too many distractions & interruptions; hard to focus on work 29

8   No before or after class meeting with other students / instructors 29

9   Lacks classroom atmosphere; or feeling of University campus life. 20

10 Not suitable for auditory learners 14

11 Feeling incompetent, inferior, stupid, inadequate, overwhelmed or confused. 14

12 Requires access to computer and Internet. 13

13 Limits certain kinds of class instruction (modelling, demonstrations, spontaneous interactions) 13

14 You have to type everything 11

15 Feeling isolated; lack of social support in studying 11

16 Team activities online are awkward 11

17 Too time consuming 11

18 Physical problems: Stiff neck, headache, lack of movement 11

19-34 Other themes (16) with fewer than 10 nominations each 74

Total nominations: 686

In sum, there are certain findings to watch especially as we do not have a blanket cheque of approval or non approval of this growing online academic environment. Those schools turning to online education in Nigeria, how equipped are they in the myriads of educational crisis in the country? What standards are in use and how have these worked out with the current situation of limited technology? In the Nigerian situation, can first degree students competently acquire requisite knowledge via online learning? Even for the graduate education online education, is the system operative in Nigeria receptive of this new wave of education? It is believed that Nigeria is still far from embracing such a feat especially as the system is scientifically under serviced and under programmed. An additional concern is the rush to obtain online certificates by Nigerians, which corroborates with the current craze for certificates. The truism is that it is partly good and partly bad in practice whether it is online learning or the certification thereof. What is the point? For Nigerians acquiring such knowledge for use in a system that has to some greater extent prepared for online knowledge base for its work force, it becomes a good endeavour. Online learning and certification in a developing education sector and economy like Nigeria will render disservice to sustainable growth. Again, online learning when imported into a totally different culture, different work condition, and different computerized system in work force, different societal ills, different infrastructural level and different mentality will be bizarre. However, imported knowledge needs to be translated into current societal conditions and systems. Our educational system has to grow to some level, stabilize and contain the work force before venturing into a debacle of online learning. More so, students who venture into online or distant education must be capable of independent academic studies. How to verify this capability and sustain it is an issue where an acceptable standard has to be created, approved and adopted. This programme of study is extensive and needs a stabilized system of education to be effectively implemented. Nigeria is not ripe for it now. Until education becomes our priority in the developmental scale of the country, this practice needs to be suspended until there is a regulatory provision in place.

iv. No Money no Education

The simple truth about the practice of education in Nigeria is that when there is no money, there is no education. There may be hidden factors to this unbecoming money syndrome in the sphere of learning. Those in government would argue that education is a government affair, that government provides free education at primary and secondary levels. More so, that government subsidizes for all federal universities. In spite of these claims, why are children of school age languishing in villages, towns and cities struggling to find means to go to school. Nigeria lacks human capital development which education provides. Is it not Socrates who said an unexamined life is not worth living? When more than half of the nation is subjected to lack of education, thus, not acquiring requisite knowledge, their life falls short of flavour. I am akin to say that education demands the lion's share in any government budget as it brings a greater number of people to some height of knowledge and understanding and responsibility. Education bridges a lot of gaps in the society.

A break down of the happenings in the country would expose the fact that money has become the bane of education without which nothing happens. One wonders why there are claims that Nigeria is a great Nation. Is it not a contradiction in terms as the education sector suffers greatly in a nation swimming in petroleum? In Nigerian history, the only time and place where free education was actually practiced was in the Western Region during the First and Second Republics. In other words, the only government that provided free education was the Action Group and Unity Party of Nigeria administrations. The Universal Primary Education of the military regime of Obasanjo was on paper, lacking in implementation. The Universal Basic Education policy is not well implemented. It has always been a false claim by State governments to have provided free education at primary and secondary school levels. Of what use would a free education be when at the side, the three tiers of the government cut corners and allow imposition of sundry levies such as PTA, laboratory and other school equipments (chalk, board, chairs, lockers, etc.), lesson, infrastructures (additional buildings for class rooms, etc.) and other developmental fees. When these abnormal practices take place, the question is, who fools who, the government or the people. Of what benefit would these side fees be to the growth of education in this moment of crisis?

Gone are the days when teachers take pride to educate pupils and students. Today it is all about money and how money can be squeezed out. Tutors no longer bother about the consequences of their ineffectiveness and its cost to the society. When teachers are poorly paid and even owed months of salaries, why would the academic system not collapse? Gravely too, leaders of the people today have nothing to show for it, they are persona non grata and are feared by the people, while producing nothing for the society. How about Senators, members of the Federal House of Representatives, Governors, members of the House of Assembly, Councillors who loot the nations treasury and of course are paid as when due? Think of the professors, teachers who taught these categories of people, who are poorly paid and uncared for. How can one right this wrong? It is a chain reaction that the education sector is turning ugly and the quality of education in Nigeria is becoming resentful. If the money provided by crude oil is not well distributed to reach all sectors of the nation's economy, especially education, Nigeria will surely collapse. There is no remedy to a systemic failure of the education sector in Nigeria with the disinterestedness of the society.

The bitter situation in Nigeria as of today is the rush to get good education outside the country. Not all can afford to study outside the country. The wealthy and the politicians can easily find the financial means to send their children abroad to study. How about others? Where would artisans, drivers, house helpers, teachers, petty traders, poor farmers, hawkers, and cyclists, lower levels of civil servants, labourers and small restaurant owners get money to send their kids abroad to study? Products of the educational system in the country, how and where do they fit in? There is a consistent cry amidst the people that the lack of education stems from a lack of money. With the literacy level very low in the country, why are the leaders comfortable with such a standard? Until this gap is bridged, there will be a continuous problem in the nation as Nigeria is currently experiencing. Disinterestedness in affairs of the nation (excluding how to steal money) by the government and its officials have paved the way for crimes, lootings, kidnappings, hooliganism, and absolute indiscipline in the society. No money no education has left the oil rich nation poorer, unhealthy, illiterate, and worse shameless.

12

Ogu I., lamented that the era of government commitment to the education of the citizenry has gone. In his article 'Before Government Forecloses the Education of Poor Nigerians' a Saharan report vividly states:

> *Nigeria's pioneer political leaders such as Azikiwe, Awolowo and Bello appreciated the value of education and government's sacred duty to provide it to the citizens. Azikiwe saw education as necessary 'to restore the dignity of man'. It is interesting that without huge earnings from oil, these leaders provided free education (in Western Region) or highly subsidized education and credible scholarship schemes and, thus, laid robust foundation for human capital development in Nigeria. (2010, Nov. 15)*

No money no education has wrecked the opportunity for brilliant children/students to further their education, improve the self and contribute to the society. And to some children, poor education has left them bereft of good knowledge and acquired skill to be somebody in the society. These outstanding and needy students turn away for lack of finance to further their education. It is pathetic, and a human right's activist and a lawyer rightly observed that the

> *Public schools have been left unattended to by the government despite the God-given resources of our dear country to provide for all. Government does not care about schools and so different heads of schools are not concerned about the falling standard and academic performance of the students. (Falana, Funmi, 2011)*

Every child should receive a decent and good education, whether he/she is from rich or poor family. Equal education is mandatory for all children and should be provided by the government. The cry of wolf by the government must stop given the resources with which the country is endowed. The three tier government has allowed improvisation to be the practice of today's schools. A trip to schools in the country would out rightly affirm with dismay the deplorable condition of schools, and that is the decay in the Nigerian educational system that lacks vision and planning. When will the use of scarce educational facilities in the country stop or to make use of only what is provided stop? These are ugly indents facing Nigerian schools, and constitute present dangers facing the education of children in the 21st century; the future is very bleak.

No money no education seems to be the gospel of the big players in Nigerian politics, while their children are abroad studying or are in some private schools of repute. The president, Senators, Governors, Members of the Houses of Rep and Assembly, the Moguls and Tycoons need to develop a strong system to ensure every child who has the talent be supported to higher education. Importantly too, no outstanding student should be turned away because he cannot pay his way for lack of money. The sooner attention is given to education with financial backing, the quicker the nation comes out from its crisis of ineptitude and lack of foresight. It may be nice to borrow a leaf from what the United States of America is doing regarding education even in the midst of economic recession. The American Recovery and Reinvestment Act of 2009 has set aside $30 billion to make schools more affordable and $40 billion for state grants. The gist here is that the Obama administration is making a long term projection, estimating that this money would enable more students to go to school, ultimately bolstering the American economy. Nigeria can do this, especially with its inherent oil wealth. There is money and there must be education provided for the citizens. Special emphasis goes to primary and secondary education; it is to the point of criminal negligence that our children are suffering from the absence of good education.

v. The Universal Basic Education (UBE)— re UPE, 6-3-3-4 education system

One is taken aback at the slow and non-working pace the Universal Basic Education is moving in the country. It is sad that

14

many children of school-age languish without formal or informal education in Nigeria. This pitiable situation is orchestrated more by the low budgetary allocations to education. An article in Daily independent Newspaper (2011) underscores that:

> *Nigeria still posts one of the highest figures of school-aged children currently out of school anywhere in the world. That is, in spite of the fact that education is seen as a fundamental human right of every citizen and the nation is a signatory to both the Universal Basic Education (UBE) programme and the target of the Millennium Development Goals (MDGs). Also, its budgetary allocation to education lies far below the 25 [26] per cent benchmark of the U.N.O. (Feb. 14)*

This confusion galore has gripped the Nigerian government and its education sector. The Universal Basic Education (UBE), formerly hatched in September 1976 as Universal Primary Education (UPE) by the Federal government of Nigeria, was a noble goal to see to the education of our children through primary level. The 1976 UPE programme was put in place by the Federal government in recognition of the dwindling education in the country after the take over of all private schools (after the civil war). This awareness generated the urgent need for national development, educational policies, educational system, programmes and changes to address the expectation of the citizenry regarding the deterioration of education in the country. The phenomenon of catching children young with quality education will definitely bring a lot of change in any country's socio-economic, educational and political well-being. The popular African phrase 'educate a child and you educate a whole village' subsists. Childhood education is always viewed as very important, and all hands must be on deck to see that this feat is continually achieved. Taiwo, C. O. (1986) observed UPE as:

> *A great contribution to education in Africa and of immense benefit to Nigeria in mobilizing its human resources, adjusting its educational imbalance and providing for the*

Nigerian children equal access to education. With constant attention and support the programme should achieve its objectives. (p. 175)

This UPE programme encountered a lot of problems and failed to bring the anticipated educational outcomes. Its objectives were not met, it was poorly executed and it lacked manpower. Fafunwa, B. (1986) observed that the UPE programme failed to meet with the national educational objectives due to some national inconveniences including financial problems, insufficient competent teachers, over crowded classrooms, narrow curriculum content and high rate of drop-outs. Adepoju, Adunola and Fabiyi, Anne revealed that in the primary education sector:

12% of primary school pupils sit on the floor, 38% classrooms have no ceilings, 87% classrooms overcrowded, while 77% pupils lack textbooks. Almost all sampled teachers are poorly motivated coupled with lack of community interest and participation in the management of the schools.

It is with this confusion that Universal Basic Education (UBE) of 1999 was conceived and introduced to satisfy the quest to fulfil the Millennium Development Goals (MDGS).

However, the period between the 1976 UPE failed programme and the UBE programme of 1999 saw another shift to 6-3-3-4 educational system in response to agitations for a better educational system in the country. This system as already mentioned above include six years of primary education, three years of junior secondary education, three years of senior secondary education and four years of university education. This system was borrowed from the United States education system. After years of practice of this educational system, it has failed due to the inherent problems in Nigeria as aforementioned. Today there is another clamour to bring a new system of education to address the failure. What a rip-off, as the nation scams itself.

Nigeria as a member of United Nations (UN) has the obligation to fulfil the Universal Declaration of Human Rights to the right to free education for all in elementary and primary stages of school life. And with the pressure of Millennium Development Goals (MDGs), another twist to education surfaced in the name of Universal Basic Education (UBE). Academic education in Nigeria will wear a new look as free education is increased to three more years as against UPE six years. First six years of primary school and three years of junior secondary education are ear marked as beneficiary years for this programme. In this light, the National Policy on Education (NPE 2004) defines basic education:

> *Basic education shall be 9-year duration comprising 6-years of primary education and 3-years of junior secondary education. It shall be free and compulsory. It shall also include adult and non-formal education programmes at primary and junior secondary levels for adults and out of school youths. (Section 3)*

The UBE programme is a welcome and desirable programme, which in 1999 the federal government in its implementation guideline specified, the following objectives:

1. Developing in the entire citizenry, a strong conscientiousness for education and a strong commitment to its vigorous promotion.
2. Provision of free Universal Basic Education for every Nigerian child of school going age.
3. Reducing drastically the incidence of drop out from the formal school system.
4. Catering for young persons, their schooling as well as other out of school children or adolescents through appropriate form of complementary approaches to the provision and promotion of basic education.
5. Ensuring the acquisition of appropriate levels of literacy, numeracy, manipulative, communicative and life skills as

well as the ethical, moral and civic values needed for laying a solid foundation for the life long living.

It is appalling that the root causes of failure of the UPE programme and the 6-3-3-4 educational system now in practice have not been addressed. How now do the proponents of this UBE scheme believe that the scheme will not meet the same fate as previous programmes? The problem is that the Nigerian practices seem not to make good assessments to past events.

To say that there is no positive input to ensure success of UBE, would be unfair to the government and its instruments for the efforts put into the scheme all these years. However, it has not succeeded as expected with the problems besieging full implementation of UBE programme. The old problems are still there and unless they are tackled the current UBE scheme will also be a colossal failure. In a paper presented by Obong, I. J. O, Secretary General, Nigerian Union of Teachers (NUT) to the 47th annual conference of Science Teachers Association of Nigeria (STAN) held at Calabar from 13th-19th August, 2006, he enumerated seven challenges facing the UBE programme, viz.:

a) *more than eight million children 6-11 years are not in school*
b) *Drop-out rate in primary school is 9-3%.*
c) *Transition rate to secondary school is 61%.*
d) *UBE program is in dire need of more than 40,000 qualified teachers, 336, 467 additional classrooms, 336,144 additional chairs and tables and 950,430 units of toilets to meet the present requirement.*
e) *Fast tracking the process of getting States that are lagging behind in accessing the UBE intervention fund.*
f) *Employment and retention of teachers of good quality.*
g) *Tracking Federal funds to ensure effective and efficient utilization.*

The truth is that the UBE programme like other programmes/schemes is failing in the areas of planning, funding, proper utilization of provided funds, provision of equipments and instructional materials, infrastructural facilities, thorough implementation, use of N.C.E teachers, good monitoring, and report on overall evaluation. This is the confusion and the predicament of today's UBE programme, and the government seems not to be anxious about it. More so, one notes that there is "a high level of uncertainties, which is beclouding meaningful planning in Nigeria's educational system. This can be very dangerous particularly as the future of Nigeria and Nigerians will be determined by the level of education her nationals have acquired" (Aluede, 2006, p. 97).

Chapter Two
Handicap of Today's Education

The botched growth of education in Nigeria during the Civil War and in the '70's left a vacuum to be filled in the educational polity of the nation. Government took over schools with no interest of developing the structure but for the satisfaction of control. What gave the long lasting blow was the fact that the country was under military regime for many years, in addition to the military undemocratic processes, marked with dictatorship, silent elimination of insubordination, and ripping off of the economy. The persistent cry by well informed citizens, especially on the products of the nation's schools and universities, created a wave of impasse. But thanks to interrupted military regimes by republican governments and finally the new democratic government evolving today, the education sector seems to be coming alive. It has been long dead and struggling to come out of its demise. The sad truth is that the whole system has fallen apart. A look at the statistic below tells how far Nigeria has flourished in education.

According to a survey by the British Council, Nigeria was supposed to have 16 million students in the secondary schools by 2008, but the number enrolled was 5.8 million,

20

suggesting that only 36% of children of secondary age were in school (Nasir, 2011).

Again, Nasir continued to explain figuratively that, "out of 1.3 million candidates who wrote the Unified Tertiary Matriculation Examination in 2010, less than 10 percent secured admissions into Nigerian public universities!".

Many factors contribute to the protracted failed educational system in the country. The undeniable truth is the fact that the viability of this country will depend largely on the sustainability of the education sector and how teachers and students alike are treated. For Ukeje, B.O, Akabogu, G.C, Ndu, A. (1992):

> *One of the greatest social problems facing most of the so called Third World nations today is the rapidly increasing demand for education on the face of steadily decreasing resources for education. This has necessarily increased awareness of educational planning and the problems of implementation in education. (p. 420)*

i. Establishment of schools—poor equipment and staff, religious battle, political egoism, good intention—poor personnel and poor execution

The take over of all previously existing private schools by the federal government after the Nigerian Civil War, created vacuum in the educational system of the country, thus necessitating grounds for the establishment of new schools. When government take-over of schools became counter productive, private organizations, individuals and cooperate bodies made formidable moves to government and gained access and permission to once more establish schools. The story of schools is that most universities are owned by federal government; a few of the universities are State owned, with scanty private universities in the country. In the Nigerian Primary and Secondary schools system, one witnesses government and private owned schools. Primary education starts at six years of age. Pupils of primary school graduate with First School Leaving Certificate after six years of education. Primary school pupils take Common Entrance Examination to qualify for admission into Federal or State owned secondary schools. Secondary school education lasts for six years, split into two, the junior (JSS 1-3) and senior (SS 1-3). In the secondary school system, at the end of first three years, students take the junior secondary school exam called the JSS3 exam. This qualifies junior students to enter senior secondary school and to be technically competent to work in the society would one choose to discontinue with education. While senior secondary students graduate with West African Examination Certificate (WAEC) and National Examination Council (NECO). However, senior secondary school students take General Certificate of Education (GCE) in their second year (though not mandatory), as a preparatory exam to their senior secondary certificate exam (SSCE). University education ranges from four to six years of academic work depending on one's area of study.

The abysmal factor to schools establishment is the inexistent scrutiny that exists. For certain, there is the white paper on schools establishment that ushered in many private and government schools. Established schools have over the years lacked necessary pruning or monitoring to introduce updates in the system. Again, since the take over of religious schools, many schools sprang up from various religious bodies. Though this is positive, many religious bodies lack a good educational foundation. The situation registered a kind of squabble among religious bodies to have schools whether prepared or not. The resultant effect is the establishment of schools with an understaffed personnel, poor equipment, manifest religious battle, and political egoism, good intention for schools but poor personnel and poor management. There is no long term planning, no good school leaders, and no maintenance. Products of the schools are below standard. In this difficulty, students are forced to undertake extra mural classes to meet up with the approved academic syllabus. The danger is that poor families who cannot afford to send their kids or register them with one of the extra mural schools for extra classes lose out.

Things have fallen apart and the education sector needs to be reformed. One may not wish to argue that money interest is the basis for schools establishment, yet, it cannot be ruled out. Public schools are meant for all but private schools are for those who are ready to spend on personnel and infrastructure to ensure quality education. The growth of private schools has put some balance to the failing public school education in Nigeria. Not only this, private schools brought competition and healthy academic rivalry, as well as underscoring the deficiencies in the education sector. The government must provide a solid syllabus that is constantly updated with a view to determining the standard for every school. Any good school must have necessary instructional materials, well trained teachers, healthy academic environment, interested parents and responsive students and pupils. The ensemble of this is government legislation on schools establishment, providing guidelines and enforcing them for academic standardization.

School administrators at all levels of education must coordinate both teachers and students in a manner that will achieve the purpose for which they are in school, as well as to help them grow into good citizens. Balance must be created between theory and practice, between school and community life. Administrators must see to it that the educational system is audaciously followed, infrastructures maintained, and teachers monitored to enliven the students' life. Buttressing this point, Starratt, R.J (1996) admonishes:

> *Administrators must constantly think of the education of the whole community of youngsters in the school. This requires them to think of the scope and sequence of all of the learning activities occurring in the school, not simply as a collection of activities, but as activities that comprise a unity, a balance, and a harmony, activities that make up a fitting education for human beings living in this moment of history, in this society, who are preparing for a challenging and demanding future. (p. 6)*

In this way, the good intentions, the responsible personnel and the excellent execution is upheld in the school system.

ii. Understaffing, product of institutions, staff aberrations

One of the greatest misfortunes any school/institution can experience is to be understaffed. Educators have continued to query governments and private owned schools on this issue. It is like the heart of the body. Teachers are needed to keep the school functioning very well. Subjects or courses must be taught and need the expertise of teachers or lecturers to get them done. Some factors militate against full staffing, namely, releasing funds for hiring of more teachers, getting well-read teachers in various fields of education especially in sciences. Nigerian is at great danger and loss especially as at

> *Present, Nigeria has about 117 Universities—owned by the Federal, some states as well as private individuals and organisations. Available data indicate that most are poorly equipped and grossly understaffed. According to the Consortium for Advanced Research Training (CARTA), instead of an academic staff requirement of 45,000 teaching staff, there are 33,000—a shortfall of 12,000 academic staff in our universities. Worst still is the fact that about 12% of the existing manpower is age and may soon be retiring, while the quality of replacement are falling (Nasir E., 2011)*

Most of Nigerian schools are understaffed, especially schools located in remote towns and villages. Teachers shy away from going to remote or local towns and villages to pick up appointments or postings; some do not even apply to such areas. Enough time should be taken to create incentives to attract teachers to such inner places. Other minor factors to understaffing of schools include lack of accommodation, towns and villages posing difficult situations, notorious and cultic schools or institutions. It is presupposed that teachers in Federal or State government owned schools/institutions possess National Certificate of Education (NCE) or a Bachelors Degree (BA) or Masters Degree (MA) to Doctor of Philosophy (PhD), and should invariably be paid appropriately. In some situations, schools/institutions are understaffed due to low Federal and State budgets for education, lack of incentives, and insensitivity of school/institution leaders to staff emoluments, as well as irregularities in payment of staff salaries and payment of preserved ghost workers (none working persons).

Understaffing does not mean only number of teachers available, it includes unqualified teachers hired to teach students or pupils. Students who passed through such illegitimate tutors would be poorly educated and their standard will definitely be low. If one could make out time to access progress of education or academic growth in the country, the result would be heartbreaking. It would attest to mass failure in public examinations, examination malpractices, and poor quality of graduates from tertiary institutions. Equally, some public and private schools do not take time to scrutinize certificates of those they hire. Sometimes, this group of unqualified personnel would settle with whatever pay/salary is offered. The problem is that when a teacher or lecturer does not possess the requisite knowledge, students under such teachers suffer. Not only that these students are deprived of the right knowledge, they are incapable of passing any external examination. Such students are continually subjected to unending extra lessons as a result of missing requisite knowledge. When the required academic background is not present, a student cannot go beyond the impacted knowledge. Students remain products of the institution. Even when that student finishes from the school or institution, passed or pushed over, this limitation will follow the person and he/she becomes one of those poorly hatched from school or institution.

Of great importance is the need to enhance the academic status of teachers as this would help to improve staff standard. It would be good to revisit the revised National Policy on Education

(1981/1986) which states in section 58 that education should be carried out inter alia:

> a   *"To produce highly motivated, conscientious and efficient classroom teachers for all levels of our educational system."*
>
> b   *"To encourage further spirit of enquiry and creativity in teachers."*
>
> c   *"To help teachers to fit into the social life of the community and society at large, and to enhance their commitment to national objectives."*
>
> d   *"To provide teachers with intellectual and professional backgrounds adequate for their assignment, and to make them adaptable to any changing situations, not only in the life of their country, but in the wider world."*
>
> e   *"To enhance teachers' commitment to the teaching profession."*

Invariably, this would assist in proper staffing of a school or an institution if adopted and practiced. Teacher education in Nigeria must meet with standardization, encouragement and investment. Policies made towards these are either not implemented or they are obsolete. The review and upgrade of teacher education would append to formal growth, enthusiasm and love of the vocation.

The destructive instrument in school system is staff aberration. When a teacher goes outside of the scheme of things to be taught, it delays requisite knowledge at the appropriate time. Some tutors do not follow the national syllabus as stipulated. This makes student fall short of covering areas mapped out for a particular subject or course. In the bid to cover up, students are tasked to read further untaught materials. Brilliant students can easily pick up but some average or below average students would find it difficult to comprehend. Thus, such students lack the knowledge due to teacher's fault. Most difficult or incomprehensible is the aberration of staff engaging in business or petty trading to the detriment of students for whom the staff is being paid. A lot of factors can contribute to this, more especially poor wages on the part of hiring body or gross insensibility on the part of the tutor. Education authorities must make out time to address such an academic disaster, as it contributes to the dwindling of education in Nigeria.

Other aberrations may include staff using students for their own studies to the expense of class work and scheme of work. Instances of change of scores or marks in academic records, and teachers making use of students projects speak loud of some of these anomalies. Secondly, further education of staff should be exclusively an in-service training or out of class academic pursuit on personal accord. It would really be hard to combine teaching and pursuing further education at the same time, as one would suffer immensely. Learning is a progression that must be respected and taken seriously. Thirdly, being on strike has become a routine and welcoming stance in the education sector. One wonders the actual number of weeks students stay in school and prepare for exam, or even are promoted to another class. Teacher Unions, Academic Staff Union of Universities and Labour Unions are not disturbed on the loss created by strikes and counter strikes. The emoluments of teachers and workers should not be withheld or delayed. Non-payment or delay in payment of salary amounts to nonchalant and negligent teacher attitude to school education. There should be round table conference and dialogue to sort things out when disagreements ensue. And collective bargaining cannot be ruled out in this process to ensure equity and proper discharge of duty.

iii. Under funding of schools/institutions, infrastructural problems

There is no out rightly gain saying that funding gives any school or institution its foundation as it opens the door for development. Schools must be built, classrooms apportioned and properly demarcated. Schools' infrastructure, qualified teachers, laboratory equipments and chemicals, libraries and reference books, brings good name to any school/institution, as they create awareness and attract parents or students to enrol. Inadequate funding of education has contributed enormously to the low quality of education at all levels, especially as improvisation (struggle to make things work even with nothing) has turned a practice. Funding of education needs to come from the different quarters namely the government, the community, business enterprises, tuition, and other sources depending on the range of school involvement in the society.

Under funding of schools/institutions have created enormous problems in the education sector and something needs to be done to truly address this matter. Olamosu, Biodun (2000) highlighted that:

> *Poor funding of the universities and other tertiary institutions has been identified as a fundamental cause of crisis afflicting our educational system. The situation is even worse at the elementary levels where teachers of primary and secondary schools are not being paid for months, where students are to provide their own lockers and chairs, where most of the buildings are dilapidated. Structures that had been erected for over forty, fifty years are not being replaced.* (p. 13)

Some have argued that funding is not the only problem of the education sector, but is one of them. If there is good budgetary allocation for the education sector and a clear means of implementation, through these processes and with proper distribution of resources there are bound to be corresponding increase in quality of education. The growing awareness of democracy in Nigeria today is yielding some good in education. Concerned citizens can now openly discuss and request for a school system that will benefit the citizenry. Some State governments map out huge sums of money in their budget for education, promising and advocating for better tomorrow. How far this is implemented is totally another untold story. This however means there is some progress seen today in the education sector. The unfortunate thing is that the mapped out fund most often does not reach the grass roots or the people for which it is intended.

There is no doubt that it is not everyone who can afford to go to private school. In other words, private schools are not meant for Tom, Dick and Harry because of its financial constraint. Establishment of private schools are for lovers of education (if one can presuppose that), who are willing to spend for education. Personal or family choice of school and spending largely depends on quality of staff, infrastructure and education. Notwithstanding, funding must be an indispensable option for erecting schools else, the proprietors are not prepared for the venture. Monetary gains would be secondary in the cadre of priorities, when eventually established schools take off and stabilize. Yet one would expect the government to critically look at the entire education policy with a view to addressing noticeable trends of today to ensure quality of education.

Choices of schools are left with parents to make, unless where the student is properly aware of what he/she wants. However, parents should be oriented on how to make choice of schools for their wards. One may not see the need for parents to have their children admitted in a school with dilapidated structure or lacking personnel. Based on the above paragraph, private schools are for parents who are willing to go out of their way to provide excellent education for their children. Since private schools/institutions in Nigeria are rather expensive, public schools remain the base for all students to gain entrance. Most parents, even the poor among them move their children away from public schools because there is no active teaching going on. And some parents in their frustration make the great mistake of sending their children to do apprentice work as alternative. Some parents, because of their grave penury condition and inability to connect for any apprenticeship for their kids, have no option other than to allow their children be where they are in public schools. For certain, this is failure for the government though no body seem to care. This therefore, calls for Federal and State owned schools/tertiary institutions to be catered for and thoroughly funded. All levels of government must consider education important, and should in spite of its lean financial resources expend on construction of new schools buildings, rehabilitate some schools of science, rehabilitate dilapidated structures in schools/higher institutions, and staff these schools/institutions even government should pay Junior School Certificate Exam (JSCE), General Certificate of Education (GCE), West African Examination Council (WAEC) and National Examination Council (NECO). This will revitalize the educational zeal and encourage students to read right and get it right. The situation is such that Odia, L. O and Omofonmwan concluded that:

> *In some states for the past ten years, not even a single structure had been added to the existing one or a significant maintenance, repairs or replacement of learning facilities and equipment rather the responsibility of school ownership and funding is being shifted while playing down on expansions of facilities to meet the demand of increasing population (p. 85).*

Today Nigerian universities are lacking in funds to develop structures and research equipments, have more lecturers and constitute research bodies. Not withstanding this problem, more universities have been introduced because of the teeming population of students seeking admission into university. More universities truly are needed but there are ways to unravel this demand via expansion of existing institutions. Problems besieging existing universities have not been addressed, it is on the increase and this process leaves more universities included in the crisis. Agbu Ifeatu (2011) argues in line that:

> *The need for more universities notwithstanding, the President of the Academic Staff Union of Universities (ASUU), Professor Ukachukwu Awuzie frowns at the rush to set up new ones. He warned that establishing new universities without commensurate funding would be counter-productive and argued that existing universities could have been expanded to achieve the same objective.*

As much as it is good to establish new universities, existing universities should be expanded and funded. The Nigerian population is ever on the increase.

iv. Low salary structure, no teacher incentive, lack of teacher education

When government allocation to schools is low, the tendency is for school leaders to maximize available resources. Standardized way of payment most often is lacking. Federal schools have more attracting income for educators than State government schools. This has generated crisis. Secondly, there is stampede to get into federal schools because of better remuneration. State government salary structure for educators differs according to the State one works with. One queries the inability of the government to regularize salary structure. This no doubt, if properly addressed would eliminate untold hitches found in services rendered by educators. The minimum to which a teacher salary should be is yet to be determined.

Low salary structure can be a silent killer of education. Some educators have resorted to business or other forms of trading or business to make ends meet. Government should be sensitive enough to address this issue with better payment structure and with accompanying restrictions for the good of the nation's education sector. It can never be forgotten that education stands for knowledge and the future of any country lies therein. Whatever will promote education at its different stages should not be taken for granted. When educators' satisfaction is sought, especially if their remuneration is proportional to their input in the society, there would be level head for productivity. Good salary scheme brings effective tutoring, commitment to duty, excellent scores, and more patriotic citizens. The effect of this borders on qualitative out-put of teachers. It should be every one's concern that quality of education rises and teachers play vital role in communicating high level knowledge, meeting up with stated curriculum. Teachers should be well trained and remunerated, if the government believes that education is critical to the development of any nation. Albert Einstein once said that, 'it is the supreme art of the teacher to awaken joy in creative expression and knowledge'.

On another note, one would question why some educators sell themselves to schools when they know that they are under paid. Contrary to what they are supposed to be to the school educators, they are far from endearing themselves to institutions that hired them. This is unfair to the schools, to the students and to the parents who labour to see that their wards receive good education. A trained teacher should not sell himself/herself because he/she is seeking for job, and ends up a failure to his/her life ambition to be an educator. This indicator is often seen in private schools. However, one wonders why a good teacher should condescend to accept just any salary immeasurable to his productive ability. One may not claim ignorance of the protracted unemployment crisis in the country as de facto a major problem leaving teachers no choice but to survive. The effect is that low salary does not leave schools/institutions with good academic environment nor with better or responsible staff.

An unplanned education system has helped to destabilize the education sector. Teachers seem to be worse off in salary, worse off in respect by parents and students, disregarded by the society and scorned by the government. Yet teachers are the foundation on which schools are built and without them the Nigerian education sector will be perpetually crippled. Teachers are usually neglected by the government and other stakeholders. It is a sad story and very odd in the history of education in Nigeria. Incentive programmes are lacking to boost the morale of teachers.

Teacher education is one other major area where attention is not given by the government who should establish such programmes for quality education. Teachers at all levels of education are not motivated to excel and update themselves to deliver more current issues in the classroom. This has led to continuous degeneration of education standard and a serious embarrassment to the education sector and Nigeria as a whole. It is a painful situation. The National Policy on Education articulated policies for the teaching profession which is good but were not backed with funding. The effectiveness of the policies is in question especially its implementation. There are stories of forgery of certificates and unqualified people manipulating their way into teaching profession. The result of this is poor teaching, bad result on external exams and poor quality of education. The growth of educational system is very much dependent on the quality of teachers and financial commitment of the government to teacher education. This entails elaborate support to education sector. This has not taken shape, as all the government proposals and assurances are defensive mechanism, buying more time to achieving nothing. There should be mentoring system for the teachers. This, when applied, will assist new teachers in their teaching and handling of students in the classroom. This definitely would help in promoting quality and maintenance of academic standard. Experienced teachers are to play mentors to the new ones.

v. Lack of keen interest by schools/institutions stakeholders—govt., churches, private bodies

Stakeholders in the education sector must be overtly involved in the affairs of schools. The Federal and State governments have monopolized policies regarding education in the country. This has always generated bickering, sidelining, abandonment of policies and neglect of ideas and closed up forum for dialogue. Stakeholders should rise to their feet for the sake of the future of education in the country. Government should include and not exclude other contributors to educational growth in the country. Restructuring education policies, formation of education budgetary allocations, implementation of set goals for the education sector, need the participation of stakeholders like federal, state, and local governments, religious bodies, teachers, parents, corporate bodies, academics, unions and interested individuals in education.

A reawakening of stakeholders' involvement in education is a necessity. Again, redefining roles of education's stakeholders to salvage the precarious situation of education in Nigeria is of paramount importance, if there is hope for the nation's education to move forward. Stakeholders must come together to get rid of substandard schools. Revisiting schools' policies established by the government with all stakeholders in education would be a step forward.

When stakeholders work together, lapses would be less in the implementation of schools' policies, and set goals would be effectively achieved. A monitoring system would be in effect and educators would take responsibility of their actions. Without much ado, working together stands as arrangement to sanitize education through the myriad of agreed guidelines. The issues of screening, registration, purchases, school environment for conducive teaching and learning, security of school, safety of students and staff, provision of recreational facilities, classrooms and ventilation, administrative offices, teaching facilities, adequate classroom furniture, workshops/seminars, involvement of educationists, curriculum and other necessary school equipments would be resolved for healthy educational system and quality education.

A change of event in the Nigerian school system is the proliferation of private schools. Private schools are where the action is for now. Stakeholders in private sector have seen the great need not to allow education in Nigeria to fall beyond repair, knowing that good educators abound in the country. Private schools are the current good schools today in the country. Private schools are of good essence, providing vital stimulus for the development of quality education. Though there are private schools that are not properly constituted or organized, and whose vision is solely to make money out of the venture. Such schools should be closed. Agbu Ifeatu (2011) advises that, "the government should also set irreducible minimum international standards for private universities, some of which are really no more than glorified secondary schools where anything goes as long as they collect their unmerited high fees." Monitoring is very important in this instance for stability of education and quality production. Many proprietors of private schools pay their teachers, lecturers, and professors well, something to emulate by the federal, state and local governments. In turn these educators in private school enterprise put in their best by the schools' standard and take the challenge of research. These schools have academic materials, good libraries, quality school administrators and best of teachers, lecturers and professors. Again, the stakeholders on this sector are not properly monitored as they extort a lot of money from students. A regulation for proper monitoring should be put in place, to checkmate excesses in this thriving industry.

vi. Cultism in schools, inability of government/ school administration/parents to stop the practice

Today, no one questions the existence of cultism in schools/ institutions. The question is, what have they done again? Fear grips parents when at last they send their kids to schools in remote places or outside their living vicinity or to live in hostels. Uncertainty to what may happen within the school frightens school leaders, especially where cultism has engulfed students' lives. Nigerian education is beset with cultism, a very big social vice. To say that cultism is in Nigerian higher institutions is an understatement; it's practically in many schools today, even in Secondary Schools. The menace experienced by cultism in schools has sent so many students and innocent people to untimely deaths and lasting wounds, and eventual drop out of school.

Cultic movements or bodies exhibit defiant and diabolic acts, anti-social behaviour, enthronement of ugly performances and blood oath relationship. This group mostly engage in nefarious and nocturnal activities, terrorizing teachers, students, parents and the neighbourhood with their unholy demands. No doubt this practice has its ugly root in the society and has had series of negative impart on learning and discipline in schools.

The sad story about inevitability of cultism in the system is the involvement of not only students but educators in institutions. Cultism in institutions has been made illegal, yet some people continue to join secret cult and have its devilish practices in operation. The reason why students join this ugly group, include protection, security, fame, responsibility, aspirations and satisfaction, belongingness, and recognition. And why nefarious activities, the usual answer will be to find their way, to intimidate and to get their mission accomplished not minding the consequences. One would see Machiavellian principle adopted here, justifying the end, not minding the means. This is a destructive principle in operation, and it is worst in the politics of the nation with lots of killing being reported and perpetrated by these people.

The unending stories of sad events by cultists bring one to ask if such a body has out grown school authorities, stakeholders and the government. Safety in our schools is inevitable for students and for learning environment. Cultism is cancerous and the entire society has to jointly put up resistance to its existence. Individual schools must make strong regulation regarding cultism and follow through. Subventions, if possible, can be provided for tackling of this ill in our schools. There must be an extra attention given to this in order to have it uprooted by the government, schools, parents, school unions and the mass media. Teachers and students should be encouraged to expose members of secret cults wherever and whenever. The society at large should be educated on the ills of secret cults, its miserable activities and its repercussions. In schools' orientation, visual messages of consequences of cultism in education should be presented and flyers distributed. In an informed and technological society of today, an expelled student of cult cannot be admitted to any other school unless with satisfied rehabilitation papers from an accredited body or person.

vii. Western brain drain

In today's global society, a big controversy arises trying to analyse Western brain drain. Be it as it may, brain drain simply means flight of growing number of highly skilled personnel in varying fields of education to the Western world. Western world in this instance interpreted to include United States, Europe, Canada, and Russia. This is flight of human capital with technical skills, talents, vision and knowledge. It is a well known fact that there is an exodus of such people leaving Nigeria for greener pasture. This running away of knowledgeable persons from the country is tantamount to reduction of best of the best in a developing country like Nigeria. Circumstances driving people away include higher salaries, security, provisions of basic amenities as rights to the citizenry, better education and job opportunities. Universities, Colleges of Education, Federal Polytechnics graduates, have over many years consistently migrated to other countries.

This emigration of personnel is seen more among graduates and those already in work force in Nigeria. It tells more about the country Nigeria. The entire Nigerian populace must be concerned with brain drain. Brain drain has threatened the fabric of this nation and is hurting the economy and competitiveness of Nigeria. It is certain that if the great brains are to be involved in the country's affair lasting changes would have occurred. These great heads are constantly praised in other countries for their talents and contributions to the societies where they have fled to. Nigerian highly skilled persons have helped to shape other countries especially the Western world. Shall the authorities and citizenry fold arms and allow this to continue endlessly?

What is happening to Nigerian education sector is similar to the unbecoming act of siphoning the nation's wealth to foreign banks by rich Nigerians. The sad effect is the non-committal, collective disregard and government negligence to the withdrawal of scholars and brains to the Western world in particular. Government can re-think this disgrace by restructuring and building anew a long term education. The school system is in total bad shape. The exemption of few good schools cannot afford to satisfy the cravings of millions of students seeking good education. Job opportunities are lacking, new jobs are not created via industries, schools, good trading relationship with other countries, expansion of government multi purpose offices and new endeavours.

Why would Nigerians not run away where there is absence of social amenities, sporting activities, electricity, and road network, bridges, provision of pipe borne water, religious tolerance and education? Nigerian students have constantly left for good schools and better education opportunities to other countries. That means, Federal Government value for education is never a priority. These students are future brains to help develop the nation. Oweto F., in his paper "Nigeria tops in school enrolment in US" reported that "Nigeria still leads other sub Saharan African countries, whose citizens are studying in the United States". He went further to clarify that, "a total of 6,568 Nigerians were enrolled in regionally accredited institutions in the US for 2009/2010 session." In an earlier statistics, an article in the Daily Independent Newspaper (2011) states that:

> *The paradox was worsened further, when in January 2010 it was revealed that Nigerian students in United Kingdom and United States totalled 20,090 and their parents spent a whopping N137 billion in tuition fees in both the 2007/2008 and 2008/2009 academic sessions. The resultant twin evils of brain drain and capital flight, though traceable to the inclement education system foisted on Nigerians by the rapacious military era of the mid-eighties, is yet to mitigate some 12 years into our democratic dispensation. (Feb, 14)*

Further, Nigerian Vanguard Newspaper (2011, April 7), reports:

> *London—Nigeria is ranked fifth among 20 countries who top the list of those with highest application for students visa into the United Kingdom between 2005 and 2010. . . . The report titled, "Student visas," obtained by the news Agency of Nigeria (NAN) on Wednesday in London, indicated that a total of 54,096 student visas were issued during the period. Further breakdown showed that a total of 6,856 visas were issued in 2005, 7,036 in 2006 and 8,385 in 2007. The report further showed that 9,666 visas were issued in 2008, while 11,205 were issued in 2009 and 10,948 in 2010.*

Most of these students stay abroad after completing their studies. The issue is lack of employment for them when they come home. Invariably, the implication is massive brain drain in Nigeria. Not only that the Nigerian financial resources are thrown away to the gain of other countries, the country losses money, personnel, and future nation developers. The migrated intelligent and enterprising students are yet to come back. Nothing attracts them home. The system has failed them. For some who have the country at heart, they are not encouraged by the happenings in the Nigerian polity. When some brave it to come home, they cannot contain the multi faceted crisis in the country. Worst today is the growing insecurity, the bombings, killings and kidnappings, to which some people who came back home experienced. Why then should the brain drain not continue in the face of all this truncated living in the country?

The effect of Western brain drain has shown in the reduction of the quality of education in recent years in all levels of schooling. When experienced university teachers continue to migrate to countries where they are offered better wages and security, Nigeria would continue to dwindle and decay. Education is suffering a lot in Nigeria. The school system has lacked incentives to improve performance, equip working environment, clear vision and control over working condition, regulated system of payment, and funding of education. The present government under Goodluck Jonathan assured the Nigerian people that:

> *His administration will turn the brain drain in the university system to brain gain, by providing a conducive environment for dedicated and qualified Nigerians in the Diaspora to return home and contribute their worth to nation-building, particularly in the education sector.*

This is an optimistic goal that should find its ground in the Nigerian polity.

viii. Misplaced priorities, literacy and community education

Part of the mishap in the country is misplacement of priorities. If education is the life wire of any country, it should be given primary attention. Generally speaking, the Nigerian government is guilty of misplaced priorities. Parents may have little blame in misplaced prioritization but greater portion of the blame goes to the three tier government piloting the affairs of the country. Any nation that really wants to develop must invest in education as both short and long term projects. At the time of independence, Nigeria had reasonably good education for its citizens but it slipped out of its leaders' hands when indigenous leadership started handling the governance of the nation. It was a gradual fall because education was never prioritized by our leaders.

The nonchalant approach of the government to educational issues would be considered as cause to some students' laisser-faire commitment to learning. Because education was not prioritized sufficiently, students' attitude to learning affected the quality of education. According to Callahan J.F (1972):

> *A person who is emotionally upset, irritated, sluggish, restless, tired, indifferent or saddened is usually not ready to learn in the classroom, talk more of doing home exercises and learning on their own. Indiscipline among pupils and students results in low educational quality. (cf F. E. Arong, M. A. Ogbadu, 2010 p. 72)*

In line with this argument, S.M.O buttresses that, "the causes of indiscipline are planted in the home by parents, watered in the schools by teachers and harvested by the society at large" (cf F. E. Arong, M. A. Ogbadu, 2010 p. 72).

Due to misplaced priorities by the government, the education sector has continued to experience strikes and closure of schools for months. This is a grave underdevelopment in education sector that has left many Nigerian students no option than to find a way to travel abroad for studies. Dr. Dauda S. Dauda (June 2003), in his article on "Misplaced Priorities and Claptrap Policies" laments on the situation saying:

> *When more is spent on the presidential fleet than on agriculture, and the budgetary allocation to a national football stadium surpasses that of our universities, one really begins to wonder what the government's priorities are—if at all it does have them.*

Arguing further on this Dr. Dauda S. Dauda narrated the IMF representative for Nigeria, Dr. Mark Tomlinson as noting pointedly that:

> *80% of Nigeria's annual income, which runs into something close to 15 billion U.S. dollars, is being expended on running the government, leaving a mere 20% to cater for agriculture, education, healthcare, security, transport, and the execution of capital projects for 99% of the country's population"*

On a disheartening note, the website on 'Nigerian Curiosity' highlighted troubling education indicators confirming that:

> *In 2009, Nigerian Universities were shut down for 5 months, affecting an estimated 10 <u>million students</u>. It was no surprise then, that 2009 saw some of the worst exam results for Nigerian students. Only <u>25%</u> of Nigerian students passed the Senior Schools Certificate Examination (SSCE) and a stunning <u>98%</u> of Nigerian students failed the NECO. (<u>www.nigeriancuriosity.com</u>)*

Further, the Federal House effort to put ban on foreign education for official's children is an indication of inability to solve the growing problem. This also speaks eloquently on their inability to address the odds in the society. Is it not painful that those who are supposed to lead do not know what to do? Is it not also an indication that those elected to lead are not qualified? Has it not also shown that the essence of political position is not to help develop the country as to what money the actors can make out of it? So, where has adequate funding for Nigeria's dilapidated education sector gone to or at least to engage educationist on which way forward? Funding of education in Nigeria has always been below expectation. Nigerian Curiosity website continues to reveal that:

> *Nigeria previously apportioned N210 billion for the education sector in 2008, N249 billion in 2009, and only N295 billion in 2010 budget. This amount is far short of what is necessary to adequately educate students and prepare the nation's workforce to be competitive on a global scale. This failure to make education a priority is further troubling because 23 million of Nigeria's youth are currently unemployable and 10 million northern children beg instead of go to school. (www.nigeriancuriosity.com)*

Literacy and community education have also lost their focus in the education sector. If formal school system is neglected, how can non-formal education thrive? It is important to know that the concept and approval of non-formal education in Nigeria was a bold step that lacked implementation. It has suffered tremendously for lack of poor quality of programmes, lack of space, unqualified staff, no incentives, high drop out rates, gender and zone disparity, and societal unchecked crimes. How does one think that the targeted group would accept to immerse their energy in a program that is neither monitored nor supervised? The targeted group is non-traditional learners including large number of street children, learners in Koranic schools, nomads, migrant fishermen and their families, etc. Imagine this crisis, neither formal nor non-formal education prosper in Nigeria. Which way forward Nigeria?

ix. Endemic corruption

My frank and honest opinion is that anybody who can say that corruption in Nigeria has not yet become alarming is either a fool, a crook or else does not live in this country. (Achebe, C., 1983, p. 37)

To say that there is corruption in the education sector would be an understatement. To say that corruption has eaten deep into school system would come close to understanding the predicament of today's education. The entire nation has fallen prey to this corrosive sickness called corruption. This acidic corruption has permeated all aspects of the Nigerian society. When the society is corrupt, every other functioning part of that society gets the pinch of it. It is therefore important to know that:

What happens to society at large affects the educational sector and whatever happens in the educational sector affects the society at large. Those in the educational sector learn and adopt predominant values generated by society at large and the society at large learns and adopt predominant values generated by the education sector. (Torulagha P. S., p. 1)

What are these corruptions in education sector? It is not far fetched, but it is the undoing of the nation and what a shame. Such are,

    a.   failure to use education budgetary allocations by school administrators at all school levels;

    b.   sourcing fund with school's/institution's name without rendering account,

    c.   inappropriate amassing of wealth by professors, lecturers, teachers, and others involved in school management,

    d. diversion of money meant to renovate infrastructures, to equip laboratories, to improve transportation, to pay salaries as when due, to sponsor educators on seminars, to be used for research, etc.,

    e. siphoning money meant for new structures, development and school/institution social activities,

    f. awarding contract with kick back, and it does not matter if the contractor can deliver or not,

    g. collaborating with contractors to provide low quality work and pocketing rest of the money,

    h. promotion of students who fail,

    i luring students to carnal relationship or pay money to pass the subject,

    j over charging parents or guardians on procurement of education items/materials, and sometimes not provided,

    k. conniving with fellow educators to deny students their right unless payment/settlement is achieved,

    l. forcing students to buy poorly written books because of compensation to collect from the author, or cover my back as to cover yours,

    m. students paying in order to be admitted, whether qualified or not,

    n. students paying to manipulate results and scores,

    o. not failing students who have not performed well, sometimes by settlement,

    p. no remedial programme and repeating of class,

    q. and others.

As students are hatched under these circumstances, witnessing and being subjected to all these abnormalities, what makes one think they would be better when they are thrown into the society to practice. They will practice what they have learned. And when they eventually take over the seat of governance, the monster called corruption will be enthroned as it circulates and multiplies. That is the predicament of the country called Nigeria. Torulagha, P. S laments that:

> *The educational sector today, seems to produce graduates who are not sufficiently disciplined and equipped with the appropriate academic and professional skills, hence, have no qualms about breaking the law, perpetually looking for shortcuts to amass wealth and are morally bankrupt. These developments are by-products associated with corruption in the educational sector as the society at large continues to spread corruption around.*

Corruption is a destructive social value. War must be declared against corruption beginning with inculcating the right values in Nigerian school system. The educational sector must be purged of this infectious malady. Many people entrusted with the provision of some school equipments failed to do so and never accounted for it. Some people in the education sector connive with such groups of bodies to liquidate schools. If these bad eggs in the education sector are not sacked or purged of corruption, there will be no tomorrow for Nigerian schools. Contracts should be made open and monitored by parents, churches and schools concerned. On these three bodies can this spreading omen be reduced and be followed on a long journey to be deracinate out of the system.

The Nigerian Federal Government for many years now is fighting war against corruption through Independent Corrupt Practices and Other Related Offenses Commission (ICPC) and Economic and Finance Crimes Commission (EFCC) which is a good move. To what extent this is being executed is another countless story. The sad situation is the presence of the untouchables, the god-fathers, and the exempted who wield a lot of power in the society. Only when one lost out of favour with powers that be, the person becomes liable to the ICPC or EFCC. If one does not belong to any of this group, he or she becomes subject to investigation by the accredited anti-corruption bodies. The masses can be arrested and rearrested at the whims and caprices of bodies responsible for uprooting corruption. The difficulty of the ICPC and EFCC to thoroughly discharge their duties lie with the fact of corruption in the upper echelon, which the anti-corruption bodies have no right to interrogate or question. Again, the anti-corruption bodies are not properly equipped by law and the defence counsel to perpetrators would always use the loopholes in the constitutional provision to defeat any corruption charges. Which way Nigeria?

The society is abashed with this ugly scenario of corruption and it is like everyone is crying to have it washed out or is it a crocodile tears. A lot of crimes have emanated through corruption and many more are entrenched because of it.

Unemployment is totally unchecked; in any case, the Nigerian world has no instrument in place to find out the number of unemployed people in the country. Olupona, J. (2011) opines that:

> *Unemployment has led to serious social crisis, armed robbery, religious violence, political thuggery, total insecurity of lives and property, and cultism in our institutions of learning. The increasing rate of corruption throughout all cadres of local, state and national levels of our governments and even in private sector reveals that things are getting out of hand. This troubling, and seemingly hopeless situation continues to suggest that Nigeria can no longer function meaningfully and productively.*

x. Crisis of poverty

> *Nigeria is determined to be poor. The evidence, at least to me, and quite a few others is overwhelming. Elite culture, the politics of the land, citizenship behaviour or lack of it and unjust institutions, orient our endowed land, it seems, towards poverty and the strife that comes with it. (Utomi Pat, 2011)*

The crisis of poverty in Nigeria is the dawn of all dysfunctional living in a nation blessed with plenty. Poverty in Nigeria has maimed the formation of the mind and the motivation towards education. Many Nigerians wallow in abject poverty, unable to meet up with needs such as food, shelter, clothing medical services, good drinking water, education, and transport. The relationship between poverty and its intractable hunger to education is a zero tolerance. This has shaped over half of Nigerian population and rendered them incapable of engaging in any educational setup. Many forms of sub human tendencies have developed amongst this group of Nigerians in their struggle to survive. Such forms include new modern slavery, child hawking, professional begging and subjection to inhuman activities (submission of children to sex, selling of children, killings, selling and use of human parts) all in search for food and to live for tomorrow. What is imaginarily unconceivable is that Nigeria is an oil rich country, a country predicted to be one of the most economically leading nations. A country built on wealth with many mineral resources. It is sad that:

> *The Nigerian Human Development Report 2008/09 (HDR) published by UNDP in December 2009 reports that 54-4% of the population lives below the national poverty line. But this figure has been available for some years and is based on a 2004 survey. By reference to the international poverty line of $1.25 per day, the World Bank offers a higher estimate of 64.4% for 2007. (OneWorld. net, 2010)*

Some have argued that Nigeria has witnessed a monumental increase in the level of poverty, estimating poverty level to 74.2 % in the year 2000 (Okpe and Abu, 2009). In another survey, the editorial of Vanguard Newspaper (2011, Mar 8) says;

> *Over the period 1980-1996, the proportion of poor people rose from 28.1 per cent in 1980 to 65.6 per cent in 1996. This translated to 17.7 million poor people in 1980 and*

67.1 million in 1996. With government's on-going reform programmes and poverty reduction strategies, the proportion of poor people is still very high about 66 per cent of the population, which translates to about 90 million poor people.

The poverty level has not changed for good, it is on the increase. Should another survey be conducted, a staggering figure to every Nigerian's shame would be recorded. Poverty is ruining the country and destabilizing the fabric of the nation.

There is no gainsaying that poverty is a stumbling block to development in Nigeria, especially education. Education which is known to be vital for the growth of any nation cannot be accessed by the people due to high level of poverty. The Development Assistance Committee (DAC) (2001) reports on poverty as a form of deprivation relating to human capabilities which includes, consumption and food, security, health, education, rights, voice, security, dignity, and decent work. Enough has not been done to eradicate poverty in Nigeria (though eradication steps have been taken and is appraised), poverty in the country has only been scratched. Over ten poverty alleviation programmes have been made since the end of civil war, but all these schemes failed woefully, chiefly because of corruption that engulfed Nigeria. The editorial of This Day (2011) reads:

The level of poverty in Nigeria cries out for urgent remedy. But unfortunately attempts at alleviating poverty in Nigeria have often times been mis-directed. The efforts begin with setting up of ad-hoc government agencies and poverty alleviation programmes. They end up as channels for government money to be siphoned into the private pockets of a few corrupt government officials and their collaborators.

There is no doubt therefore that the programmes introduced have left the poor poorer. The programmes are a feat yet to be achieved. No wonder, the various United Nation's—Human Development Index (HDI) reports have consecutively "ranked Nigeria very low in human development." Further, "Nigeria is presently topping the list of countries with malnourished children. Nigeria is ranked as the 20th country with the highest number of hungry people on the Global Hunger Index (GHI)" (This Day, 2011).

Mr. Peter Ujoma, a researcher, a sociologist and human resource practitioner, in his informing lecture on 'Contemporary Issues in Poverty and Nigeria's Development' discovered that there is a high risk of educational underachievement for children who are from low income home. He went further to stress that:

> *These children are often at higher risk to drop out than their counterparts from wealthier homes. High levels of juvenile delinquency, teenage pregnancies, etc, occur among this group. They often lack positive role models and often become mothers in their teens. Illiteracy increases the chances of unemployment which in turn affects income generation. (Edukugho E., 2010)*

Education which is the center of successes in any society has continued to suffer and fail tremendously in Nigeria.

More effects of poverty can be seen in the uncoordinated administrative achievements of the country. Government has failed its citizens. The masses are frustrated waiting for the government to use the oil wealth of the country to put the nation back on track. The inability of the government to address poverty has damaged the educational system, where parents would rather choose to send their children to hawk and do street trading so as to raise money than to go to school and perish out of hunger. Most children drop out of school because of poverty stricken conditions. This is a pathetic and colossal failure of the government caused by its instability and ineffective leadership.

The more pathetic situation is the hopelessness of citizens to help themselves. The blame game is always easy. Government cannot do everything. No one wants to lift a finger towards working out programmes for poverty alleviation even among those who can afford to do so. In his long but precise argument, Utomi Pat Prof (2011) hints:

> *The trouble with Nigeria is that many think it will come mainly to politicians who have done a lot, no doubt, to damage our lives, either from greed or ignorance. I see it coming to most of us; to the businessmen who will not lift their purses to encourage change, perhaps because their personal fortunes come from the misfortune of the absence of level playing fields; to middle class people so protective of their Land Cruisers they dare not speak truth to power; to policemen who allow ruling parties to convert them to uniformed thugs of the party, and judges who corruptly adjudicate; and even opposition politicians who see more of their ego than prospects of rescuing their country from bad governance when collaboration talks come up.*

The rate of unemployment in the nation is frightening and has created a large framework of non-functioning potentials in the society. Thereby, increasing the poverty level and multiplying crimes in the society. Most of the crimes in the society are committed by unemployed youths. The youths are used as thugs in political campaign, and are manipulated to do dirty works for the sake of food, drink and a token of money for politics of unreason. Painful to this is that they can kill, kidnap, assassinate, rape, traffic on human body parts, wreck peace and stability just to make some money. Graduates roam the streets looking for what to do. Most of these youngsters in frustration join all kinds of fraudulent people in order to feed. Poverty has generated a lot of bad will, frustration and anger towards any sustainable growth in Nigeria. One bemoans the fact that:

> *The primary cause of poverty in Nigeria is failure to distribute the country's vast oil revenues more equitably. Inability to develop employment opportunities through non-oil industry sectors is such that, in 2008, oil revenues*

contributed 97.5% of exports and 81% of national budget.
(Oneworld.net, 2010)

Gwegwe, kali (2011) writing on poor distribution of national
wealth and how it impacted on poverty opines that:

> *Effective distribution of national wealth will reduce the gap*
> *between the various social brackets in the country. This will*
> *mean that every Nigerian citizen will live above poverty*
> *line and indirectly discourage the culture of graft. Most*
> *cases of graft have foundation in the inability of citizens to*
> *meet the basic needs of life.*

No one can doubt the fact that the resources in Nigeria are
sufficient for the people of the country. Greed has impoverished
the nation, as few people amass the wealth meant for the good of
the entire populace leaving over half of Nigerians begging for food,
shelter, health and education.

Chapter Three
Balancing Education Ineffectiveness, need for reformation

The education sector has had a continuous degrading slope. The graphic slope has moved from 85% to 30%, counting from independence to date. There is no denying the fact that decades after independence have been a retrogressive down slope in the education sector in Nigeria. This is a very big imbalance in the state of affairs in the country. Is there any way out of this entrenched complexity and what proposals can be offered? The education sector must be reformed in order to get it back on track. The former head of State, General Yakubu Gowon, in a lecture decried that, "the situation in the nation's education sector had reached a critical stage where it would be criminal to keep quiet and watch: The alarming decline of the quality of our education in Nigeria has not been this terrible" (Tribune Newspaper, Jan. 2011). In fact, leadership and greed are prominent problem lingering in the ineffectiveness of education in Nigeria. This is lamentable. Achebe, C. (1983) believes that:

> The trouble with Nigeria is simply and squarely a failure
> of leadership. There is nothing basically wrong with the
> Nigerian character. There is nothing wrong with the

Nigerian land or climate or water or air or anything else.
The Nigerian problem is the unwillingness or inability of
its leaders to rise to the responsibility, to the challenge of
personal example which are the hallmarks of true leadership.
(p. 1)

Nigeria has multi-faceted problem embodying leadership and follower-ship. Not only that the leadership is incredibly poor and uncommitted to nation building, the followers are gullible and insensitive. This is a bad omen for a country like Nigeria endowed with human, material and natural resources. Is there any way out of this cobweb problem in Nigeria or shall the country be allowed to decay?

To expect a one year miraculous turn of events would be unrealistic and improbable. An evolutionary journey of sequential progression must have to begin in order to address this colossal defect, and consequently turn around the table for good. Restructuring is not easy but if majority agrees to effect change, it will happen irrespective of any lag or fierce suppression. Education remains the best bet to move things around; trust must be reposed on the education sector to reverse the country's unending under-development. Nigeria has lacked well educated and informed leaders. The change education brings is durable and is non violent. Epictetus is quoted as saying, "only the educated are free". Aristotle agreeing said, "the educated differ from the uneducated as much as the living from the dead". In view of this, Thomas Jefferson opines that, "enlighten the people generally, and tyranny and oppressions of body and mind will vanish like evil spirit at the dawn of a day." In sum, literacy liberates the mind as education brings literacy. The government must persist on mass education of its populace, as it will bring change that knows no bounds in the politico, socio-economic Nigeria. This must be canvassed to ensure education reform at all levels.

There is still time to move things around. Nigeria is blessed with intellectuals, academics and persons who can step up to challenge the battered situation. When such people emerge, the support of the people is needed to sort things out. However, some steps must be taken to do this tedious task, looking ahead for change. Today's generation must leave a good legacy for tomorrow's generation and there is no other way than to establish good education in the country. To do this successfully, the education sector, especially the administrators of schools at all levels of education must apply past knowledge to the present, as this would dispose them to create a good academic vision for Nigeria. The future of Nigeria is at stake, everything possible should be done to project a greater tomorrow with informed citizens. Kouzes J. M. and Posner B.Z. (1987) expound that:

> *While knowledge and experience are the resources of intuition, they are not by themselves enough to produce an ideal image of the future. Visions do not leap out of our past wholly formed. Nor is our future merely a straight-line projection from the past. Like all raw materials, knowledge and experience must first be extracted, refined, and processed before they produce usable ideas. (p. 96)*

Every individual is an embodiment of body, mind and soul, and can competently start effecting change within the self for a better tomorrow. Changing individual unwarranted views and bad idealistic tendencies may help the purging process. The world of education is the key to a better life for any country, society, community, and the individual. Attention to education would bring changes that no body would have ever imagined to happen.

i. Strict regulation on educational system, discipline

The educational system must be standardized and regulated. Since Nigeria adopted the U.S educational system of 6-3-3-4, each segment must strictly be followed. Lax should not be allowed as it gives room to other unknown factors detriment to positive furtherance of the system. There should be focus, linked to meet with the needs of its citizenry, while installing discipline and self reliance. If the government and society cannot right the wrong in education sector and the educational system, then one can as well forget other sectors of the nation's life. And if teachers at all levels of education are not qualified to render their duty, then the country's educational system can never survive not to mention develop.

Nigeria needs good leadership in all spheres of socio-economic, politico, and educational governance. The green light is given by President, Goodluck Jonathan as he advocates strict admission regulations in universities to ensure quality assurance in the education sector. In his ebullient statement in representation by the Minister of Education, Prof. Ruqquayat Ahmed Rufa'l, stresses that "in order to improve the quality of lectures in the university system . . . to ensure that universities engage in sustainable capacity building and human development programmes which will keep lecturers abreast with best practices in teaching, learning and research" (Vanguard, Jan 21, 2011). The point here is that all hands should be on deck to rectify the lost educational system. There must be ways to check perpetual breakdown of discipline, general decline of efficiency and effectiveness because of the loss of direction. Strict regulation in the educational system therefore would require this A to Z steps, namely,

a. Reforming teacher education at all levels
b. employment of qualified teachers in all tiers of education,
c. capacity building and human development programmes for teachers at all levels of education,
d. teacher licensing and revalidation of licence,
e. remuneration and benefits commensurate to the teachers' status,
f. regularized payment structure for the teachers, no debts,
g. stopping all forms of bribery, manipulations and the famous IM,
h. de-politicize education for continual quality education,
i. establishment of national quality assurance,
j. engage teachers in research for comprehensive data collection and quality access and equity in education,

k. funding by government and business enterprises, and parental/guardian tuition/fees,

l. establishment and review of school curricula for healthy schooling, syllabus at each level of education must be met,

m. fund release for construction of new schools, and renovation of dilapidated structures, investment in infrastructure at all school levels,

n. inspectors/supervisors of schools at all levels should be men and women of proven integrity,

o. strong monitoring system created, if possible an independent body,

p. defaulters to professional code to loose their teaching profession,

q. recommendation from place/s of work needed for any hiring or re-hiring,

r. established pattern of financial accountability and probity to be followed,

s. punishment for disregard for rules and regulations,

t. Purified entrances into schools/institutions and external examinations devoid of any form of malpractice,

u. Merit at all levels of school admissions,

v. Consistent academic calendar, avoidance of strikes and closing of schools,

w. number of years for graduation and remedial programme,

x. exemplary dressing and conduct, and civic education,

y. school regulations and student conduct, school discipline at all levels of education,

z. Mentors for new teachers, stewardship for the maintenance of existing schools/institutions, and so on.

It is on these above stated facts that, 'the great aim of education is not knowledge but action', said Herbert Spencer (1820-1903).

When these are observed, a development oriented, professional, competent and ready to serve education sector would emerge, capable of responding efficiently and effectively to the demands of the society. Nigerian leaders should pay more attention to the demands of the education sector, especially as all the developmental aspects of a nation are subsumed in education by the quality, competency, accountability and literacy level of the society. It is therefore, 'upon the education of the people the fate of this country depends' (Benjamin Disreali).

In his contribution, Gowon categorically calls for complete overhauling of the entire education system and restructuring of its operations as a sine qua non. He went further to suggest that this could be achieved through "a well conceived reform in order to return the lost confidence of the outside world in its quality". It would take great discipline and regulations above to achieve this feat. Indiscipline has pervaded the society in all ramifications of the country's life. This is a terrible hold on the people which has continued to create disorder, laisser-faire attitude, non-compliance, and unwarranted delays.

Today there is a serious move by the government to change the educational system of the country back to what it was before the 6-5-4 system. What the nation needs is to apply strict regulation with greater emphasis on implementation. There is nothing wrong with the 6-3-3-4 system of education, what is wrong is in the policies made towards its continual actualization. No matter what system of education is to be adopted, if the conditions above are not met, that system would fail to satisfy the demands of good education and the nation would constantly clamour for change. Kenneth Gbaji, the Minister of State for Education argued that the current system of education the 6-3-3-4 system has failed to deliver the desired benefit for which it was instituted. In his thought, he adduced that:

> *The policy has failed to address the nation's many education challenges, stressing that the country might return to the earlier 6-5-4 system next academic session. . . . He further defended the decision of the FG by highlighting additional weaknesses of the 6-3-3-4 system to include its inability to address the yearnings of Nigerians in the area of education advancement. (Odeh, Onche, 2011 Feb. 6)*

The position of Federal Government seems to be elusive and contrary to the recommendations of the stakeholders in education. Odeh Onche (2011) highlights that, "the recent announcement by Gbaji contradicts the recommendations of a recent education stakeholders' summit for the government to refocus and restructure existing education policies at all levels especially the concept and implementation of the 6-3-3-4 system of education." He went further to state:

> *although the stakeholders at that summit convened by President Goodluck Jonathan suggested that the best institutional arrangement for the management, regulation and coordination of education at all levels be determined, it did not ask for abandoning the 6-3-3-4 system of education." (ib.)*

As aforementioned, the problem of the educational system is not in changing it but in the policies guiding it and the implementation of same. If federal government goes on with new system of education, it means the government is not listening to the rest of stakeholders in education. The famous Nigerian factor is still a shadow prohibiting the country from effectively advancing the educational system. The system about to be scraped by the Federal Government works in developed nations for example United States. However, any educational system in use or introduced must have to be continually used, developed and modified to suit current day events and needs of the society. There has to be consistent monitoring of any educational system by educators and in the process up grade and up date the system continually to answer the country's day to day questions. The country cannot continue to change educational system without foresight. The problem lies in making 6-3-3-4 system a Nigerian educational system, in the sense of indigenizing it and upgrading and updating it to suit the Nigerian society. In event that a new system of education is adopted, care should be taken to allow the system understand the Nigerian structure. Secondly, day to day monitoring, updating and fine tuning must be used to sustain it. If not, tomorrow will bring another system.

ii. Not only consumers but producers

One good thing education does is to make the learner knowledgeable, productive, creative and self reliant. This is reform when placed correctly. Nigerians have had this minimally, amounting to difficulty in becoming producers. Greater proportions of Nigerians are just consumers. The little numbers that can produce are not encouraged to come forth with their skills. Why? Because nothing is in place, there is no direction, no objective as a country, no leadership, and no agreed formula of doing anything, no security for the civilians, no structured government, no amenities and in fact no order. To worsen the situation, the constitution is violated with impunity even among the custodians.

After fifty years of independence, Nigeria has no indigenous produce that catches the international body or out come of research to boast of. The nation is full of consumers who have no interest in creating a nation of its own standard. The education sector that should lead in research and experimentation has fallen short of its standard. Where would then come development? Nigeria has continued to be a nation on the receiving end. She sources finished products, looks for the most refined of all things and has perpetually been a consumer society.

Countries labelled as third world with Nigeria in the 20th century have surpassed it in the 21st century. A key reason for their growth is restructuring and in some cases overhauling of the education sector. Nothing stops Nigeria from doing this but the generated corruption, poverty and lack of leadership in the country. One would guess the nation has settled for mediocrity, because if she has reckoned with excellence, by now Nigeria would have been a country of producers.

It is amazing that everything from natural mineral resources to what we eat is stereotype of consumer tendencies. Think of the crude oil, to date, Nigeria has not been able to mine it herself. If so called petroleum scientists cannot mine, how would they engage in refining? See how other mineral resources we have in the country have just gone out of production or are under produced because we lack personnel. Such mineral resources are groundnut, cocoa, iron ore, and coal. One wonders what happened to the Ajaokuta steel industry, the Cement industries, and the Enugu Coal mine, each of which can be a major source of any country's income. The country has not indigenized these natural minerals to make them hers. The decline of education in Nigeria has done untold harm to procurement of creative minds in science and other subjects to engender new ideas that in turn will generate production. The infested evil in the society today is the incessant quest to become rich over night without education, work, or struggle in business, or endurance to rise within rank and file in office work or business.

Nigeria is barely surviving because of her dependence on foreign companies to excavate our mineral resources, refine them and bring prosperity back home. The mineral resources by nature are natural producers, while Nigerians are its consumers. The companies that refine these natural minerals are producing a consumable product, while Nigeria and other countries she sells the crude oil to are the consumers. Worst is that most of the countries buying crude oil from Nigeria are already producers and Nigeria with all the money generated is incapable of becoming a producer country. Nigeria has lost the lustre that makes a nation self reliant and that is education. There is generally a kind of slack, just like hands akimbo waiting for finished products and money accruing from it.

To restructure, to improve, if possible to overhaul the education sector will be the most singular good any government can give the Nigerian people in its predicament. "When the time for restructuring comes, managers need to take account of tensions specific to each structural configuration" said Bolman L.G and Deal T.E (2003, p. 82). The essence of education is to make students consumers and producers by the knowledge impacted. Research institutes must be established and money spent on research for indigenous findings and productions. Lots of investment must be made in education and research if the Nigerian world can compete with the rest of the world. Teachers, students, and interested bodies under control must be encouraged to go beyond the classroom into the research field. If these are put in place, and implemented among other things, primary, secondary and tertiary institutions would have more grounds for intense academic competition, more qualified teachers, and productive environment. In a nutshell, this would "rebuild a culture of scholarship which has been eroded by under funding" (Bollag, February 1, 2002, A40). This goes with the basic understanding about the standard practice of academics the world over as strongly built on research, where lecturers and students brainstorm issues. Only informed persons can develop ideas, and become producers. Uninformed persons are perpetually consumers and remain unwilling to step into the unknown.

iii. Ability to fight odds in the society

The rising tide of education is to withstand all forms of trivialities from the government and the society. Enlightened minds know when things have gone wrong and proffer solution. The educated can halt a nation for a positive change when in majority. This is a reason why the Nigerian education sector needs to be reformed. The distinction has to be made that not all who pose to be educated are really educated. Distinction must be made between let my people go group from the right way to do it group. This is why obviously not all can raise voice in disagreement to the onslaught in the society by leaders, as most hands are tied to the stake. It behoves on the unsoiled literate and informed body of the society to step up and say no to oddities in the country.

The odds in the society are there because of the lack of people with requisite knowledge and with the capacity to overcome them. Beginning with bad governance that has plagued Nigeria for many years, some groups of people have hijacked the country's leadership achieving nothing but siphoning money and disrupting true democracy to achieving personal aggrandizement. The most unfortunate were the military regimes that crippled the nation. Second, are the so called democratically elected persons that understand nothing about human freedom or choice? All forms of leadership or governance that do not synchronize with good living, development of the country and provision of necessities must be reprobated in law and in actuality. This is a necessary reform to be realized.

The Nigerian political structure is veiled with corruption, manipulation, buying over Independent Electoral Commission (INEC) officials, and recycling of politicians through political appointments, alignment and realignment for purposes of sharing money. The interest of the people is never in the equation, yet democracy is government of the people by the people and for the people. The Nigerian people should rise to their feet and fight for civic right. The pending problem to achieve this is chiefly characterized by lack of interest and low literacy level which is rated 39—51% in Nigeria (US Department of State). In the executive summary of the Federal Ministry of education for the Forty-Eight session of the International Conference on Education (ICE), it succinctly states that, "Nigeria is the only E9 country in the Sub-Saharan Africa with equally the highest illiteracy rate in the sub-region" (p. i). What a shame to the acclaimed giant of Africa and the most populous country in Africa. Agbu Ifeatu (2011) analyses that:

> *The situation in Nigeria is particularly worrisome because one would expect that a nation with vast oil wealth should use a substantial part of its resources to develop its human capital. It is indeed ironic that Nigeria, despite her oil wealth is sharing the dark basement with highly illiterate societies. A recent Global Monitoring Report on education shows that Nigeria is one of only 10 countries that account for 72 per cent of the global number of 796 million illiterate adults. It is also one of the 15 countries with more than half of the world's 23.6 million out-of-school children.*

Fighting odds in the society is a wholesome task, involving every true meaning Nigerian in order to guarantee sustainable reform. It is unknown to most Nigerians what the legislative arm of the government has accomplished since the 1999 democratic dispensation. Many Nigerians consider the House non-existent. The members are not interested in democracy but rather their pockets and how best to manipulate the system to enrich themselves. People, who were voted to serve the country, go there to loot. It is a pitiable situation engulfing the nation. The people who elected them can change them out-rightly with vote of no confidence, but how many Nigerians are politically aware. Politics of ego have swerved the governors, making service to the people irrelevant. Other political offices are as a matter of fact, how much money one can get out of it. Sad enough, there is no monitoring of functionality of these politicians or any emerging system to put to an end this globe money trotting of politicians. Who will bail the cat, especially as the few who are knowledgeable seem to be bought over with ill gotten money dangling by their side? This ugly episode is to silence the experts in allowing politicians have their way while the nation suffers. The "Ghana Must Go' episode of the political class in Nigeria has reduced the country to how much money one has or can afford to give out in bribery. With education abandoned to languish in oblivion, where then would effective change emanate?

The society is besieged with poor education, no leadership, money bag politics and high rate of unemployment. These ills account for the social malfunction and disintegration of the society. Man is a bundle of possibility, and the awful situation in the country has left the society infested with multifaceted crimes and inhuman activities viz., bombing, kidnapping, killings, insurrections, prostitution, human trafficking, stealing, break down of law and order. The short cut and long term solution to this moral decadence is by investing in education, teaching the young to know the difference between wrong and right, and engaging the youth with something meaningful. The young ones need to be attracted back to school rather than being content as apprentices to different forms of trading, yielding little or nothing to them, leaving them paupers when business goes bad or the owner decides not to financially advance his/her apprentice after many years of service and learning in the trade.

iv. Accepting knowledge not just money as power, education paves the way

Knowledge in essence is power. It is a truism that is indisputable. The power of knowledge endures and stands the test of time. It does not terminate neither is it affected by recession. Yet very few people have tapped from that source of power called knowledge. It is also true that some people have believed money is power. Money therefore must be obtained no matter the means. This is disruptive and it affects people negatively. Acquiring money without knowledge is a cheap way to fame, and it does not last. Money in itself is good, how it is acquired is a totally different dimension involving right or wrong. However, the comparison here is that knowledge takes precedence over money as an enduring factor of life.

Knowledge brought about the existence of money. Every country aspiring to grow seeks knowledge to do so. Education paves the way to know. Knowledge therefore is the one and only instrument capable at all times to fight the odds in the society. Knowledge via good education builds a nation. Warren Lisa in her expose contends that "knowledge is truly power", when she says;

> *When it comes to life in general, knowledge is power. The person who understands himself and other humans gets along better with others, understands how to care for others, knows how to get respect for himself, knows how to learn and teach, and understands any number of other things that can make interacting with others and becoming a whole person easier.*

Knowledge liberates the mind and frees one from the bondage of the unknown. Thus, knowledge at no time can be equated to money. The conception of money as power is to the extent of money one has and for what the money is used. From the Internet Archive of Marx/Engels, Goethe explicates that "the extent of the power of money is the extent of my power. Money's properties are my—the possessor's—properties and essential powers." Shakespeare from the same archive highlights:

> Money, then, appears as this *distorting* power both against the individual and against the bonds of society, etc., which claim to be *entities* in themselves. It transforms fidelity into infidelity, love into hate, hate into love, virtue into vice, vice into virtue, servant into master, master into servant, idiocy into intelligence, and intelligence into idiocy.

Money as good as it can be in procuring one's needs falls short of itself from its encumbrances. Education that leads all the way to knowledge would make money relevant but not as important to life. Knowledge therefore disposes the mind to argue persuasively, to socialize, to manage money, to be prudent, and to raise families, to distinguish from what is right to what is wrong, to understand history, to engage science and other wide range of varieties and benefits. Because knowledge is essentially powerful and useful at all times, it must be sought. A country without knowledge will crumble. The reason why education is of paramount importance is because it keeps the country strong and viable, socio-economically and politically sustainable. Thus, irregularities of all sorts need to be purged when proper education is maintained, offering the country with the knowledge base to function effectively. Thus Tross O.C. opines:

> *Education is empowerment in many ways. It has the power to eradicate ignorance, poverty, and make individuals become independent because of their career choices. In life's supermarket, we are encouraged to take education seriously because it affords us to be self-reliant.*

v. Advancement in all spheres of societal biddings/ endeavours—education, science, law, medicine, media and relationship, etc

Another move as a way out in balancing education ineffectiveness is to thoroughly diversify the education sector to include all aspects of societal life. What this means is that all relevant courses and academic programs must be vigorously taught in schools and advanced in research to engender adequate information in all spheres of human life. Academic programs like experimental sciences, medicine, pharmacy, law, social sciences, management sciences, nuclear energy, engineering, mass communication, journalism, information technology, agriculture, international relation, psychology, guidance and counselling, computer science and specialization in single subjects, would be deemed fitting. Advancement in knowledge through research provides up-to-date awareness of current information. To come out of the ineffectiveness engulfing the nation, the education sector must be strong and productive. Through this means the knowledge provided thereof, would help build the democratic systems being manipulated. It will also create political awareness and help Nigerians to analyze problems and make rightful decisions. In a lecture delivered at Caleb University, Imota, Lagos State of Nigeria, Professor Jacob Olupona of Harvard University, Baltimore, United States summarizes that youth's involvement and integration into the religious and public life as viable contributors to civil society begins with a strong education (Olupona, J., 2011). In line with this, Diogenes Laertius is quoted to have said, 'the foundation of every state is the education of its youth'.

On a broader spectrum, programs or courses on trade/ entrepreneurship are handy educational training bound to uplift the country, the individual and reduce the unemployment rate shattering the nation. No doubt, today's society wants to sit doing nothing while expecting money to come to their laps. Courses such as, Media (photography, printing, computer typist, etc), Office (data processing, computer graphics, computer designers, basic accounts, etc), Personal Care (cosmetology, tailoring, shoe makers/designers, artistry, etc), Engineering Repairs (auto body, auto mechanical, plumbing, electricians, cell phone repairers, welding, etc), Carpentry, Furniture and Decorating (Carpentry and joinery, mechanic work, upholstery, etc), Outdoors (mining, fisheries, animal husbandry, etc) and others (marketing, sales, dyeing, bricklaying, leather work, textile trade, tourism, etc), are indispensable areas to major or master. These are rare skills to possess and it yields a lot. One can be employed by the government or private body or perfectly establish self reliant work-shop. Eze Stella (2011) argues:

> *The problem of skilled manpower is the result of half-baked graduates, either from the secondary or university level. Those who graduate from the secondary level are fed into the society without any tool to help themselves, or the society, even if they cannot immediately proceed to the university. This has been attributed to the high unemployment rate, since millions of people graduate on an annual basis without the necessary skills to fall back on. Countries like China and Indonesia have taken advantage of entrepreneurship education, thereby producing graduates who are not liabilities, but job creators, to accelerate the economic growth of their countries.*

Each person needs awareness, information, and mode of doing things, which education provides and sustains. The education sector needs to be funded to meet up with the demands of students to avail themselves of the programmes that would create better vision and a new Nigeria. Consolidating on this, the Nigerian educational system would then produce qualified personnel who have critical and creative minds, who are ready to stake themselves for the course of a viable nation. This course of action ensures presence of industries, factories, research institutes, sporting facilities, entertainment fields and amenities, good health services, electricity, good access roads, availability of water and well circulated pipe borne water, clean environment, and well rounded awareness.

Today's leadership should endeavour to plan ahead and build into the system developmental programmes to enhance the social strata. Primary in this overview is education. Policies to beef up the process of nation building must be addressed and government officials guided towards its implementation. There would be no more incoherent and inconsistent policies whether in local, state or federal levels of the government. Policies should no longer be made in view of gain to make through contracts therein. It is appalling seeing the extent to which the Nigerian leadership has degenerated, so much so as to translate every thing into monetary advantage. Priorities must be set right to advance societal biddings and endeavours. Proficient and honest people committed to serve must be raised to responsibly handle affairs of the motherland. To do this, the essence of educating citizens, having durable educational system, and funding the education sector cannot be overstated. Success of nation building is tasking and requires endurance, consistency in the mission and vision a country sets out to accomplish, without prejudice to provision of day to day administration and sustenance of the society. The greatest of this success is the enduring education.

A taunting shadow pursuing Nigerians is the fact that everybody knows it better than the other person. Most people have forgotten that some people are really gifted or rather are more talented than others. Nigerian government must allow experts to work and recreate things. The mind set of Nigerians must change, it is unbelievably truncated and naïve even amongst the literate group. Strikes and counter strikes must be stopped, and a civil way of doing things needs to be reachable. Each time there is strike, the society goes back months behind because of the heinous outcome. A government that persistently refuses to pay salaries or generates pandemonium among its citizenry, should be voted out, and if possible impeached. If Nigerians can learn a peaceful way to reject government provisions or practices without destroying structures or crippling the system, that would be commendable. When people destroy structures, it is the people who would suffer as a lot would be spent again to rebuild, which ordinarily would have been channelled into new project. Non-violence is the key factor to bringing change and a lasting peace. Dr. Martin Luther King advocated for this, died in the course of it and left a great legacy of non-violence for which he is celebrated by all today. Non-violence brings a more effective change at long last. In a novel edited by Washington J. M (1992), he recounted on:

> *the positive appeal that non-violent direct action had among some black youth was evident on August 19 when members of the National Association for the Advancement of Colored people (NAACP) Youth Council conducted several sit-ins at lunch counters in Oklahoma City. (p. 29)*

vi. Patriotic orientation, changing value system

Patriotism is love for one's own country. That means one is willing to give up every thing for a nation's course. Strictly speaking, patriotism is the life wire that sustains the pride, wholeness and well being of a country. Patriotism involves everyone, whether serving in government or in the private sector, leader or follower, rich or poor, Christian or Moslem or Traditional, to give one's country a boost for a better tomorrow. It entails readiness to serve and defend one's country, cherishing indigenous products and supportive of changes that would augment the growth of the society. Patriotism has to do with positive development of the mind and the endowment of willingness to give unalloyed support through good services and relinquishing of rights for common good.

Nigerians are patriotic except for the fact that there is a whole lot of animosity, acrimony, weird behaviours, and unprecedented flair for corruption, persistent poverty and incredible individualism. These and other incorrect attitudes have warranted the call for patriotic orientation and change in value system. The orientation is not far fetched if only each individual person would put up a new outlook and behaviour to be polite to the nation's differences, dialogue brotherly and strive to contribute positively in keeping the rules of law as enshrined in the constitution. Leaders are to lead by example while the led should be good followers. Nigerian literacy level needs to be improved to enable most Nigerian people to be on the same page with development, responsibility and patriotism. In his book, *The trouble with Nigeria*, Chinua Achebe asks the question, "Who is a patriot?" He answers as follows:

> *He is a person who loves his country. He is not a person who says he loves his country. He is not even a person who shouts or swears or recites or sings his love of his country. He is one who cares deeply about the happiness and well-being of his country and all its people. Patriotism is an emotion of love directed by critical intelligence. A true patriot will always demand the highest standards of his country and accept nothing but the best for and from his people. He will be outspoken in condemnation of their short-comings without giving way to superiority, despair or cynicism. (pp. 15-16)*

Patriotism also demands the ability of every Nigerian to institute action against the odds in the society. In a broader sense therefore, changing the value system is very paramount, and speaks loudly to the hearts of fellow citizens. Nigerians can rise to their feet, and stand their ground against any tyrannical person in the society including leaders as well as followers. What change in values would do is to enlighten us to cherish those things that bind us together first as a nation before ethnic, group, personal and any other gimmick. The same old saying that, knowledge is power and that education liberates the mind and paves the way to information holds and is still obtainable.

Education is the main route out of poverty. Education opens the door wide for job opportunities either from government, private sector or self employment. It is a truism that a hungry man is an angry man. Even though lack of education is not a license to flout rules, it can be a big deterrence to meeting up with demands of the society. Without requesting too much, the Nigerian society possess the right to basic amenities from the government especially, electricity, water, access road, education, health, and good governance. Poverty, said Mefor Law:

> is *so strong that once it attacks and destroys self esteem, it asserts itself over the person's life and gradually eats him up until nothing is left. Even the physical self is eaten up by poverty, leaving often only a mass of bones covered with discoloured skin. Poverty is therefore the worst thing that can happen to a man and that is why the entire life struggles are but to escape it but majority never succeeding [ed] without intervention.*

However, patriotism is a nation's calling and all Nigerians are expected to be oriented more towards it. Patriotism transforms and brings freedom with which to move a nation forward. Patriotism seeks justice and puts citizens on the right path. Education provides patriotic actions and ensures steady growth of a nation. 'Next in importance to freedom and justice is popular education, without which neither freedom nor justice can be permanently maintained' (James A. Garfield, 1831-1881, July 12, 1880). It is therefore right to allude that, 'education is not the filling of a pail but the lightening of a fire' said William Buttler Yeats.

The entire Nigerian people should believe in their country and strive to make it grow whether one is resident at home or outside the country. Patriotic acts and good values are what the citizens should aspire to accomplish. It is also a great value to love one's country and assist to transform things for good. A lot of sacrifice is involved for a redirection or tuning one's mind to be patriotic and be a value-oriented person. One has to be cautious because there are good and bad values. The concentration of this book is on good values or good value system, and impeccable patriotic projections. Good values make a nation a repository of love, trust and oneness. Values are intrinsic to day to day beliefs and morality of the people, and therefore build a nation. A country with bad values has a dead society and nothing would ever work out well. When a value system is in place, people can distinguish what is right from what is wrong.

The nation's value system is her identity. A good value system is motivational, sustains society and promotes civility. There would be need to inculcate civility in mode of living in the Nigerian society, and introduce civic education in schools where national consciousness has dwindled tremendously. This remains the way to reformation.

Evaluation

There is no one best administrative way to do things. So also in education, but there can be few excellent ways to reform and restructure the education sector in order to have an effective educational system in Nigeria. Such excellence should be sought for and in the process up grade the system to maximally suit the cultures of the people. This book outlined strategies to help enhance education in Nigeria. It would not claim to have said it all, because research is an ongoing thing, as each day opens new ideas and new meanings. So it is with today's ideologies which may not be the ideology of tomorrow. But there is always a sequence, a follow up from previous to present, from yesterday to today and beyond. The book extends its invitation to all teachers who see to the education of children from kindergarten to university to read and follow through for a better Nigeria All stakeholders in education must of necessity play some role in reshaping the poor image of the education sector. Joint effort is needed at this critical moment in Nigerian education system. It is demoralizing to note that,

> *Today, a ranking of top 8,000 Universities in the world done last year showed only 5 Nigerian Universities in the first 100 in Africa. Our top universities were: Ilorin (55th—Africa, 5,846th—World), Obafemi Awolowo (61st—Africa, 6,265th—World), Ibadan (63rd—Africa, 6,396th—World), Jos (74th—Africa, 7,000th—World),*

*and University of Lagos (79ᵗʰ—Africa, 7,246ᵗʰ—World).
What happened? Why and where did things go wrong? And
how can we revive the most critical component in human
capital development? (Nasir, E. 2011)*

There is need for educational transformation, more hands are needed to tackle educational problems, and if possible external and foreign hands can be co-opted as knowledge knows no bounds. No one should forget that "every age and people have seemingly devised a system of education suited to their own needs and circumstances" (Ukeje, B.O, Akabogu, G.C, Ndu, A,1992, p. 1).

Educators are urged to instil into the educational system a lasting discipline. Civic education must be entrenched into the school system at all levels. In a gradual process (few years interval) the fruit of the labour shall manifest. Good education brings immeasurable changes and one can always count on it, it does not fail. Dissatisfaction with the education sector and the educational system is as old as the education itself. The country must have to move on, government has to accept alternative methods and appoint qualified personnel to assist in remodelling the educational system. If what this book laid out is properly assimilated, accepted and implemented, change will of its own accord emanate. Nigerians must not fail to recognize that the educational system is a faithful reflection of the social ideologies of the nation it serves.

Teaching is a great sacrifice which requires updating, and it is also rewarding and fulfilling. When one imparts knowledge, there is fulfilment surrounding the person for leading others to climb the tree of knowledge, an aura of actualization. Listening to U.S. President Mr. Barack Obama in the State of the Union address of January 25 2011, he emphasized and appealed to the education sector of America saying, 'if one wants to make a difference in the nation become a teacher, your country needs you'. The sharp distinction from what is obtainable in Nigeria is that in the U.S. educational system teachers are trusted, well paid, consulted, incentives created and have continuous research embedded into the system. Continuing with his speech Mr. Barack Obama cited South Korea as a place where 'teachers are known as nation builders'. This calls for emulation, as this book enjoins the federal, state and local governments to follow through. As high as U.S. is in governance, literacy, health, agriculture, international relation, etc, the government has continued to invest in education and research. This is because education and research are the future one can give any country. Nigerian leaders must learn from this and bring the country to compete with other nations of the world. In fact:

> *To actualize Vision 2020 we must toe the path taken by both India and China. We have to involve our best brains from across the globe. Government has to set the template to involve all the stakeholders, so that enough human and material resources are deployed to the development of education for the overall benefit of the nation. (Daily Independent, 2011)*

Nigeria lives on borrowed robes, adopting Western and Asian pattern of life without properly analyzed or established foundation, completely consumed in the capitalist and socialist world with nowhere to perch, lacking its own voice and style of governance. What a groundless foundation? The country is yet to make the educational system her own, and until such a time when a stable educational system is in place, an unpoliticized system of funding established, the nation's educational pain will continue to manifest and multiply. The government should make effort to create a right educational environment for learning. Education must be standardized, with teaching and learning equipments made available for effective and efficient learning. When education is satisfactorily pursued in Nigeria, a lot of growth shall be registered and the country transformed for good. Oghuvbu E. P alludes, "the major role of education is manpower development. Apart from this, the manpower developed must be able to help solve major issues our country faces. As a result education must be relevant to these issues, not separated from them". (p. 21).

For educational system to have one voice and succeed, provision of basic amenities need to be actualized viz., electricity, water, access road, a structured system. This would reduce unnecessary encumbrances withholding good education. Secondly, the nation's past history hunts and weighs down on the people. It is a hard truth, an undeniable factor that our chequered history is a monster to progress but it can be overcome with good governance and leadership. The government vis a vis good education, should endeavour to address economic conditions by creating more jobs, people earning enough livelihood to support their families and have some time to attend to their children's education. Government should ensure equitable distribution of resources meant for academic purposes. Equity in particular is interpreted to mean:

> *Fairness in sharing the resources available for schooling.*
> *This educational value corresponds to a general societal*
> *value honouring fair play and equal opportunity. Equity*
> *does not always mean providing identical resources to each*
> *student or school or providing the same access to every*
> *educational program. Sometimes identicalness and sameness*
> *are considered unfair. (Sergiovanni, Burlingame, Coombs,*
> *& Thurston, 1999, p. 7)*

The education sector must be funded to enable it take giant strides to turn education in the country around. In a recent budget discussion, it is interesting that the Senate laments of the decadence in the nation's education and is canvassing for N500bn bail-out bond to help the education sector with needed funds for its repositioning. The chairman of the Senate Committee on Education, Senator Uche, Chukwumerije clearly states:

> *Lamenting that the education sector was not just*
> *deteriorating, but was in shambles . . . the sector required*
> *a master plan. He blamed the sector's plight on decades of*
> *wrong prioritisation, warning that the long neglect of the*

sector would '. . . sooner than later, confront our future
with a grim harvest'. (Akogun, Kunle, 2011)

Attention should be given to many students who take Joint Admission and Matriculation Board (JAMB) but cannot be admitted due to limited number of universities. More universities need to be built, existing ones maintained and funded. It is unfortunate that while one mourns the backwardness of education in Nigeria, those who are interested to gain more knowledge do not have institutions to absorb them. Meanwhile the country's population is on the rise. In a recent drive by the President, Goodluck Jonathan, about nine more federal universities have been approved in six geo-political zones of the country. Certainly, Nigerians would applaud this progress. It is not enough, as the government needs to do all it takes to put everything about education as priority. Even if another round of universities is established it will not take the teaming population of students seeking admission into tertiary institution. Another worthy move should be to expand existing universities and to fund them appropriately. Oyekanmi, Rotimi L. (2011) summarizes:

Indeed, access at the tertiary level has been a major
challenge for various administrations. Every year, between
800,000 and one million candidates sit for the Unified
Tertiary Matriculation Examination (UTME), but the
spaces available are less than 200,000. While applications
to Polytechnics and especially Colleges of Education have
been low, preference for the universities has been increasing.
Parents who could afford to, have been sending their
children to European and American institutions, and lately
to the few Universities in Ghana. (The Guardian)

Learning is not attained by chance. It must be sought for with ardour and attended to with diligence said, Abigail Smith Adams.

When there is imbalance in education the society suffers. So it is pertinent that the Nigerian child be given good education to alleviate further deterioration and disintegration. The sending of children abroad by rich Nigerians to study would not solve the tentacle spread by bad education and uncaring attitude of government. The unalloyed truth is that the children of the rich and the poor alike, those who could afford decent education for their children and those who cannot afford it are the future of this country. There would be vicious turmoil if care is not taken to offer the future generation basic quality education. These children would rise to fight each other, maim and obstruct progress. So blatantly put by Barrister Falana Funmi:

> *A society that does not manage its educational sector properly like ours is preparing to increase the level of illiteracy, mediocrity, poverty and chaos in future! The children of the poor who are in the majority and who have been denied the right opportunity and quality education will definitely rise up against the children of these privileged ones and deny them peace later. The future of the so-called rich parents think they are securing for their children is not secured at all.*

The corruption in Nigeria comes into question even in the education sector. This must be trampled and those found wanting on this should be reprimanded or at some point dismissed to allow new prospects to hold. Nigerians should know that, "money as the existing and active concept of value, confounds and confuses all things, it is the general confounding and confusing of all things—the world upside-down-the confounding and confusing of all natural and human qualities" (Marx/Engels). Corruption is a substantial problem in Nigeria and it is a major constraint to national development, and it is a core factor to the malaise of education in Nigeria. However, 'the very spring and root of honesty and virtue lie in good education' (Plutarch, 46 AD-120 AD, Morals).

The Nigerian government has so much to do to boost education. Since the system is crumbling, and many ideas are out there to be sourced, government should form an independent committee of experts to work out new educational strategies to enhance an existing system and possibly embark on completely new pattern. There is urgent need to do this, bearing in mind that the existing school system must not be completely washed out. Ogunmola, Dele and Badmus, Isiaka Alani concur that, "government should establish credible and efficient institutions for proper resource management, while the existing ones need to be strengthened" (p. 13). Nigeria has the money to invest in education and should endeavour to meet with the UNESCO's standard of 26 per cent allocation to the sector. No argument is more important other than to say that as education is a tool for human development, the nation's growth anchors on literacy level it has attained.

The Nigerian nation must tap from its pluralism, and emphasize benefits therein. Together as Nigerians we break through, together we achieve and together we build a strong nation politically, socially, technologically, religiously and economically. Let the pluralistic nature of the country not be a weakness but strength to fathom all problems and jettison as well as incarcerate all hatred. Education is the one and only, and the surest way to attain the goals of nationhood. Education is the greatest of all reforms; reformation of the sector is a sine qua non for Nigeria.

About the Author

Alphonsus Emeka Ezeoke is a priest. He has served the Church in many capacities at home and abroad. He is experienced in administration and social fields. He has travelled wide. As a scholar, he acquired Degrees in various fields—Philosophy, Theology, Public Administration and Education. He is a Board Certified Chaplain (BCC) with the NACC, a Professional Body in the U.S.A. He is also a PhD holder in Educational Leadership, Administration & Policy from Fordham University New York.

References

Achebe, C. (1983), *The trouble with Nigeria*. Portsmouth New Hampshire, Heinemann Educational publishers.

Adepoju, A., & Fabiyi, A., Universal Basic Education in Nigeria: challenges and prospects.

Agbu, I. (2011), *Nigerians deserves quality education. Nigeria* Masterweb Daily News—Publish Yourself, 28/03/11. http://nigeriamasterweb.com/blog/index.php/2011/03/28/ nigerians deserve quality educat . . .

Akogun, K. (2011), *Education: Senate Canvasses N500bn Bail-out bond*. Thisday Newspaper, 08 Feb 2011.

Aluede, R. O. A. (2006), *Universal Basic Education in Nigeria: matters arising*. J. Hum. Ecol., 97-101. Kamla-Raj 2006.

American Federation of Teachers (2001), *A Virtual Revolution: Trends in the Expansion of Distant Education*

Arong, F. E., Ogbadu, M. A. (2010), *Major Causes of Declining Quality of Education in Nigeria from Administrative Perspective: A Case Study of Dekina Local Government Area*. In Canadian

Social Science, Vol.6, No, 3, 2010, pp 61-76. ISSN 1712-8056. www.cscanada.net www.cscanada.org.

Bollag, B. (2002), *Nigerian universities start to Recover from years of violence, corruption, and neglect, the chronicle of higher education.* Feb. 1, 2002, A40-A42.

Bolman, L. G. & Deal, T. E. (2003), *Reframing Organizations: Artistry, choice and leadership.* Third Ed. San Francisco California, John Wiley & Sons Inc.

Catholic Bishops Conference of Nigeria (2006), *The Communique: Catholic Education in Nigeria Within the 21ˢᵗ Century.* First Catholic Education Summit in Nigeria. Nigeria, Austine Diamond Enterprises—08034532615, 2006, Feb 7-9.

Daily independent Newspaper (2011), *Getting the education system out of the doldrums.* Nigeria: Feb. 14.

Dauda, D. S. (2003), *Misplaced Priorities and Claptrap Policies.* Ternepol, Ukraine, June 2003. In www.nigerdeltacongress. com/marticles/misplaced_priorities_and_claptra.htm.

Development Assistance Committee (DAC) (2001), *Rising to the global challenge: partnership for reducing world poverty. Policy statement by the DAC High Level Meeting upon endorsement of the DAC Guidelines on poverty reduction.* Paris, 25-26 April.

Dike, G., & Otti, S. (2011), *Interview with Okpala, NECO registrar.* The Sun news online. http://www.sunnewsonline. com/webpages/features/education/2011/feb/01.

Edukugho, E. (2010), *Nigeria: Expert examines damaging effects of poverty, corruption on education.* Nigeria: Vanguard Newspaper, April 28, 2010.

Eze, S. (2011), *New senior secondary curriculum introduced in Nigeria.* Nigeria, Leadership Newspaper, 17 March 2011.

Ezeoke, A. E. (2003), *The governance structure of an archdiocesan schools office: politics and policies.* U.S: MI, Ann Arbor: UMI 3084910.

Fafunwa, A. B. (1974), *History of education in Nigeria.* Revised edition 1995. Samadex Nig. Commercial enterprises ltd (printing division) Ibadan, Nigeria.

Fafunwa, A.B. (1986) *Perspectives in Nigeria education system.* London: George Allen and Unwin Ltd.

Falana, F. (2011), The *condition of public schools.* January 28, 2011. In www.thisdaylive.com/articles/the-condition-of-public-schools/85471/.

Falola, T. (1999), *The History of Nigeria.* Westport, Connecticut U.S: Greenwood Press.

Federal Ministry of Education (1981), *National Policy on Education.* Lagos, Nigeria.

Federal Ministry of Education (1981/86), *Revised National Policy on Education.* Lagos, Nigeria, 1981/86.

Federal Ministry of Education (2004), *National Policy on Education.* 4th edition (NPE) NERDEC, Yaba—Lagos, Nigeria.

Gwegwe, K. (2011), *Nigeria: Problem of poor distribution of national wealth.* Nigeria: Nigeria Masterweb Daily News, Feb. 18.

Gowon, Y. (2011), *Gowon laments rot in education sector.* In Tribune Newspaper of Nigeria. January 22, 2011.

Jonathan, G. (2011), *Nigeria-Education: Jonathan advocates strict admission regulations in universities.* In Nigerian Vanguard Newspaper, Jan 21, 2011.

Kouzes, J. M., & Posner, B. Z. (1987), *The leadership challenge: How to get extraordinary things done in organizations.* San Francisco, California: Jossey-Bass Inc., publishers.

Makama, D. S. (2011) *Nigeria's population to hit 166 million by October, says NPC.* http:www.ngrguardiannews.com/index. php?option=com_content&view=article&id=5419

Marx/Engels Internet Archieve, *Karl Marx Economic and Philosophic manuscripts 1844".* http://www.marxists.org/archive/marx/works/1844/manuscripts/power.htm.

Mefor, L. (2010), *Psychological effects of poverty and implications for patriotism in Nigeria.* September 5, 2010. http://elomba.com/index.php?option=com_content&view=article&id=3930:psychological.

Nasir, E. (2011), *Why Education Can't Wait.* ThisDay Live, July 29 2011. http://www.thisdaylive.com/articles/why-education-can-t-wait/95888/

Nigerian curiosity website, www.nigeriancuriosity.com/2010/04/ban-on-foreign-education-for-officials.html.

Obong, I. J. O. (2006), *The State of Basic Education in Nigeria: the way forward.* Calabar, Nigeria: A presentation. http://www.nutnigeria.org/state_primaryedu.html.

Odeh, O. (2011), *Discarding 6-3-3-4 education system.* Nigeria: Daily Independent Newspaper.

Odia L.O., & Omofonmwan, S.I. (2007), *Educational system in Nigeria problem and prospects*. Development center, Benin City, Nigeria & Ambrose Alli University, Ekpoma, Nigeria. J. Soc. Sci., 14(1): 81-86, Kamla-Raj 2007.

Oghuvbu, E. P. (2007), *Education, poverty and development in Nigeria: the way forward in the 21ˢᵗ century.* Abraka Nigeria, Delta State University. J. Soc. Sci., 14(1): 19-24, Kamla-Raj 2007

Ogu, I. A. (2010), *Before Government Forecloses the Education of Poor Nigerians Saharan\Reporters.* 2010, Nov. 15. www.saharareporters.com/article/government-forcloses-education-poor-nigerians.

Ogunmola, D., & Badmus I. A., *Meeting the challenges of the millennium development goals in Nigeria: problems, possibilities, and prospects.* Australia, University of New England, Armidale, NSW 2351.

Okpe, I.J, & Abu, G. A. (2009), *Foreign private investment and poverty reduction in Nigeria (1975-2003).* J. Soc. Sci., 19(3), 205-211.

Olamosu, B. (2000), *Crisis of education in Nigeria* Ibadan Nigeria, Book Farm publishers, 2000.

Olupona, J. (2011), *Nigeria at the crossroads: Religion, education, and nation-building.* Nigeria: The Guardian Newspaper, Feb. 14, 2011.

OneWorld.net (2010), *Poverty in Nigeria.* Nigeria: March 2010.

Oweto, F. (2010), *Nigeria tops in school enrolment in US.* November 19, 2010, 12.40am, http://234next.com/cms/sites/Next/Home/5644014-146/nigeria_tops_in_school_enrolment

Oyekanmi, R. L. (2011), Questions, intrigues over new varsities, visitation panels. Nigeria: The Guardian, Feb. 17.

Sergiovanni, T. J., Burlingame, M., Coombs, F. S., & Thurston, P. W. (1999), *Educational governance and administration (4 ed.)*. Boston, MA: Allyn and Bacon

Starratt, R. J. (1996), *Transforming educational administration: Meaning, community, and excellence.* New York, NY: The McGraw-Hill Companies, Inc.,.

Sun News Publishing (2011), *Varsity education and NUC's cross-border model.* http://www.sunnewsonline.com/webpages/opinion/editorial/2011/feb/01.

Taiwo, C. O. (1986 reprinted), *The Nigerian education system: past, present & future.* Lagos, Nigeria: Nelson Pitman ltd.

The Federal Ministry of Education for the Forty-Eight session of the International conference on Education (ICE, 2008). *The development of education: national report of Nigeria.* Theme: Inclusive education: the way of the future Geneva, Switzerland. November 25-28, 2008.

This Day Newspaper (2011), *Nigeria: Napep and poverty eradication (Editorial).* Nigeria: Feb. 14.

Torulagha, P. S., *The Corrosive Effect of Corruption on Nigeria Educational System.* http://www.gamji.com/article6000/NEWS7987.htm.

Tross, O. C., *The power of Education 101.* http://ezinearticles.com/?The-power-of-Education-101&id=2768513.

Ukeje, B.O, Akabogu, G.C, Ndu, A. (1992), *Educational Administration*. Enugu, Nigeria: Fourth dimensional publishers.

U.S. Department of State (2010), *Background note: Nigeria*. November 1, 2010. http://www.state.gov/r/pa/ei/bgn/2836. htm.

Utomi, P. (2011), *The poverty conspiracy*. Nigeria, THISDAY LIVE, 26 Feb 2011. http://www.thisdaylive.com/articles/the-poverty-conspiracy/86869/

Vanguard Newspaper (2011), *Wanted: A President for Nigeria's poor*. Nigeria, Vanguard, Mar 8, 2011. http://www.vanguardngr. com/2011/03/wanted-a-president-for-nigerias-poor/

Vanguard Newspaper (2011), *Nigeria ranked 5th on UK student visa application list*. Nigeria, Vanguard, April 7, 2011. http://www. vanguardngr.com/2011/04/nigeria-ranked-5th-on-uk-student-visa-application-list/

Warren, L. H., *Is knowledge truly power?*. http://www.helium.com/ items/363526-is-knowledge-truly-power.

Washington, J. M. (1992), *Martin Luther King Jr. I have a dream: writings & speeches that changed the world*. New York, U.S: HarperCollins publishers.